D1458391

The Food Almanac

Volume II

RECIPES AND STORIES FOR A YEAR AT THE TABLE

By Miranda York

ILLUSTRATIONS BY JORDAN AMY LEE

PAVILION

Contents

Introduction

If you're returning to *The Food Almanac* series – welcome back! I hope the first book carried you happily and hungrily through the seasons. As we're already acquainted, feel free to dive straight in.

If you're new to this series, let me share a little more…

To put it simply, this is a book about good things to eat. It's also a collection of brilliant food writing by some of the most talented cooks and scribes, from legendary food writers and lauded chefs to up-and-coming poets and debut novelists. You'll find memoirs, essays, short stories and poems alongside recipes, menus and monthly reading lists, presented within the framework of a seasonal food almanac: a month-by-month guide to the culinary year. Each chapter begins with an introduction to the month ahead, followed by seasonal highlights for the larder, spotlights on ingredients and passages on food history. The chapters end with a menu, each recipe carefully chosen to show off the best of the season, and a reading list, should you wish to delve deeper into the ingredients explored and the stories told.

As you may have guessed, this is not a traditional almanac. It won't tell you about the tides and the phases of the moon; it won't list the times for sunrise and sunset, or suggest when to sow seeds and harvest crops. It will tell you the best time to eat each harvest, though, and I hope the following pages will intrigue and inspire, weaving practical advice and recipes through stories that are at once universal and intensely personal. This is not a manual, dictating and reprimanding, but a book about enjoying food. It's about cooking in harmony with the seasons, how it can be a pleasure, not a chore, and following the rhythm of the growing year. There's a sense of anticipation as the landscape changes around us, and joy to be had from the bounty it brings.

I hope this alamanac will be both a companion in the kitchen and a book to curl up with; that you'll enjoy the literary musings on food, cook the recipes from the monthly menus and perhaps learn something new along the way. Cooking, eating and feasting with friends are threads that run through all our lives, a tapestry connecting us to the past and present, as well as the world around us. Take a seat at the table and join the conversation.

A Note on Seasonality

The seasons cannot be rigidly defined; they are unpredictable and ever-changing. Apply a similar attitude to the way you use and interpret this book, flicking to the chapters either side of your chosen month for recipes and culinary inspiration.

In each chapter, you'll find a list of seasonal produce, followed by a spotlight on one of these ingredients. These lists draw attention to some of the highlights of the season, a quick reference to provide instant ideas when you're shopping for your supper. The lists lean towards British produce, though there are specialities from our neighbours, too. With the exception of forced produce (such as rhubarb, radicchio and sea kale), they refer to fruit and vegetables that mature outdoors without artificial heat or shelter. You'll also discover wild foods to forage from the fields, woods and hedgerows.

Most fruit and vegetables are now available all year round, whether it's because we've found clever ways of extending the seasons, or because produce is shipped from the other side of the world. The hard edges have blurred and the idea of seasonality has been all but forgotten. Yet there's something special about dipping spears of asparagus into soft yolks in spring, biting into the perfect peach in summer, gently moving wild mushrooms around a pan frothing with butter in autumn, and peeling a jewel-like blood orange, its citrus mist thrilling the senses, on a grey winter's day. Eating with the seasons brings a rich variety to our lives and is, of course, more sustainable. But most satisfying of all, it tastes better.

MIRANDA YORK

January

A month for staying put, slowing down and revelling in the rituals of the kitchen. The fields and hedgerows may look bare but January can be surprisingly abundant. Delight in the colourful citrus fruits and bitter leaves – fresh and vibrant flavours after weeks of festive indulgence. Marmalade on toast for breakfast, lentils for good luck, tonics and teas for cold days, and a cake fit for kings.

IN SEASON

Black mustard leaves	Kale
Blood oranges	Lemons
January King cabbage	Radicchio
Jerusalem artichokes	Seville oranges

Seville Oranges

Bitter oranges arrived at our tables long before their sweet cousins. Early cookbooks calling for oranges in both sweet and savoury recipes referred to the bitter orange right up until the beginning of the nineteenth century. Far too sour to be eaten fresh, they were prized for their sharp juice and aromatic peel, their elegant tartness often appreciated above lemons.

While bitter oranges still feature in Latin American and Middle Eastern cooking, it's only in Britain that Seville oranges are obsessively sliced, squeezed, de-pipped and boiled into marmalade for a few short weeks at the beginning of the year. We are devout marmalade-makers, importing almost the entire crop (some 4 million kilograms) grown around the southern Spanish city. It has even been suggested that Sevilles would fade into obscurity if it wasn't for our bittersweet addiction. Perhaps this far north we're more in need of the warming glow of these little pots of preserved sunshine – an annual celebration of citrus to brighten our kitchens and lift our mood.

Delicious as it is spread on buttered toast, there are more inventive ways to use marmalade – try it in a bacon sandwich, alongside cheese or swirled into a Swiss roll. Look beyond preserves to make the most of the fresh fruit, too. Nothing equals the perfumed juice in baked orange creams, jellies, fools and ice creams, and the zest makes cakes and tarts sing. Turn to the past for sharp takes on familiar recipes: squeeze into sauces for white fish, such as turbot or brill; add to marinades for duck, pork and lamb; steep the zest in alcohol to make ratafias or shake up your cocktail repertoire with Seville orange margaritas.

MAKE AHEAD

Vin d'orange

If you're buying Sevilles for marmalade, save a few to make this elegant Provençal aperitif. Mix rosé or dry white wine with sugar, vodka, vanilla pods and sliced bitter oranges, then leave to infuse in a cool, dark place for a few weeks. Strain, bottle and let the flavours mellow for as many months as you can resist. A silky, bittersweet aperitif to look forward to in summer.

A VERSATILE FRUIT

The fragrant blossoms are harvested for orange flower water, used for millennia in sweet and savoury dishes throughout North Africa and the Middle East. The aromatic oil extracted from the thick peel flavours liqueurs such as Cointreau, Curaçao and Grand Marnier.

WHAT TO DO WITH SEVILLE ORANGES

- Whisk the juice and zest into a dressing with olive oil, honey and garlic, then drizzle over broccoli or thinly sliced raw kohlrabi.
- Pickle sliced red onions in the juice for topping tacos.
- Use your homemade marmalade as a glaze for roasting ham, or make a traditional Cumberland sauce for gammon or game.
- Try a different citrus preserve – a bittersweet Seville orange curd is a delight.
- Switch lemons for Sevilles in the classic Sussex Pond Pudding.
- Make mini jellies – bright and sharp – to serve after a hearty meal.
- Squeeze into rum punch or make a refreshing homemade orangeade.
- Add a little juice to dark chocolate ganache and roll into truffles.
- Preserve in salt using the same method for preserved lemons.
- Freeze the zest and juice – or even the whole fruit – for use later in the year.

Bitter

by Russell Norman

It is no coincidence that when Italians want something to wake up their taste buds and sharpen their appetites they reach for a bottle of Campari, Cynar or Fernet Branca. These aperitivi all share the essential quality of bitterness that is so important to the national palate, the elusive *agrodolce* theme that defines much of Italian cooking. The Venetian classic *sarde in saor*, combining sweet onions with sardines and vinegar, is the perfect example of an everyday route to bitterness and sweetness. Serving salsa verde with grilled meats has the same purpose. And nowhere in the vegetable kingdom is this more pronounced than in the thrilling chicories of northern Italy.

Radicchio, as the humble chicory is known in Italy, comes in many varieties, shapes and colours. But the unifying quality is bitterness. In my mind, there is a kind of pecking order, a hierarchy of flavours, that rises like a glorious crescendo.

We start with Castelfranco, a pretty radicchio from the region of the same name. Its delicate leaves give it the appearance of a flower, butter-yellow with subtle pink and red striations. I always think it looks like a Missoni pattern, and it wouldn't surprise me if the Milanese fashion house took its inspiration from this beautiful plant, sometimes fancifully known as winter rose or orchid lettuce. Castelfranco works wonderfully well with toasted hazelnuts and a light dressing of extra virgin olive oil and lemon juice. I find it irresistible whenever I see it on the market stalls of enlightened greengrocers.

On the next rung of the ladder is the round, red Chioggia radicchio, the size of a small melon, the leaves curled tightly around the central ball. It's a great addition to big, crunchy salads, shredded and tossed with a heartier dressing of olive oil, red wine vinegar and a large teaspoon of Dijon mustard. Chioggia is the radicchio that's easiest to find outside Italy, and it has the longest season, gracing the shelves from October to March.

The flavour profile of the torpedo-shaped Treviso radicchio is even more pronounced. Deep red with pale, creamy veins, the best way to prepare Treviso is to slice it in half lengthways, drizzle with olive oil, salt and black pepper, roast in a medium-hot oven for 20 minutes and then shower with microplaned Parmesan and chopped flat-leaf parsley. It's wonderful as an accompaniment to grilled red meat or game, or eaten as a hearty starter.

But at the top of the class, revered for its beauty and subtlety, is the Tardivo (meaning late), so called because it grows and is harvested much later in winter than its siblings. Tardivo is a joy to behold, with long purple fronds that look, to my fanciful mind, like a small octopus in flight, shooting through the water to avoid a potential enemy. The vegetable requires careful husbandry to produce those distinctive vertical leaves, picked after the first frost to guarantee optimum bitterness. It is miraculous in a red wine risotto, though often I simply eat it raw with olive oil, salt and a little lemon juice. Of course it is more expensive, but worth every extra euro.

Intensely bitter flavours may not be to everyone's taste – I have seen the confused expressions of those who try Campari for the first time, or eat my signature dish of puntarelle with anchovy dressing – but I'm a teacher by trade, a restaurateur by profession, and an educator by nature, and I'll continue to fight the agrodolce fight until I've converted everyone I know and love.

Tonics and Teas for Cold Days
by Rachel de Thample

TAHINI COCOA

Comforting as a down feather duvet, this version of hot chocolate is also stress-soothing. The magnesium in cacao calms the nervous system, while the herb brahmi, a staple of Ayurvedic medicine (easily sourced online), provides additional mental health benefits and lends an earthy undertone. A touch of hygge to embrace on a chilly winter's day.

Serves 2

4 tbsp tahini
4 pitted dates
3 tbsp raw cacao or cocoa powder
1 tsp brahmi powder (optional)
1–2 tsp rose or orange blossom water (optional)
1 tsp ground cinnamon
A fresh grating of nutmeg
500ml (18fl oz) plant-based milk, organic dairy milk or water

Blend everything together until smooth. Pour into a saucepan and gently warm through. Pour into mugs, cradle and sip.

LEMON DROP ELIXIR

A tonic to support the immune system. Limonene, a compound found in the peel of citrus fruits, helps reduce inflammation, and the gentle aromatics of cardamom and cinnamon pull their weight therapeutically too: cardamom supports the liver in eliminating toxins, while cinnamon is antibacterial and antiviral.

Makes 500ml (18fl oz)

1 whole unwaxed lemon, quartered
6 cardamom pods
½ tsp ground cinnamon
500ml (18fl oz) filtered water

Place the lemon quarters (zest, pith and all) in a high-speed blender with the cardamom, cinnamon and water. Blend until smooth. Scrape through a fine-mesh sieve into a jug to remove any fibrous, pulpy bits and pour into a clean bottle. Store in the fridge for up to a week. To stave off colds, you can drink this either gently warmed or topped up with fizzy water as a tonic.

BLOOD ORANGE AND GINGER TISANE

Like Sevilles, January is the season for blood oranges. Including these vitamin-C-rich fruits in our diet boosts the immune system. Ginger aids digestion and also increases blood circulation, which in turn keeps you warm. The fresh bay leaves accentuate the aromatics and complement ginger's digestive powers.

Serves 2

1 blood orange, cut into 1cm (½in) slices
2 tbsp freshly grated ginger
2 fresh bay leaves
300ml (10fl oz) freshly boiled water

Add everything to a teapot and let it steep for 5 minutes before straining into teacups.

DANDELION OAT LATTE

Dandelion root has the most incredible smoky, coffee-like flavour notes and it's a great caffeine-free alternative to a shot of espresso. It's also a brilliant source of antioxidants, vitamins A and C, and minerals including potassium and zinc – rich, vital nutrition for the winter months.

Serves 2

2 tbsp ground dandelion root
½ tsp ground cinnamon
250ml (9fl oz) freshly boiled water
250ml (9fl oz) oat milk

Add the dandelion root and cinnamon to a cafetière and pour over the freshly boiled water. Brew for about 5 minutes. Warm the oat milk in a saucepan until steamy. Pour the dandelion coffee into mugs and top up with the milk.

Couronne des Rois

by Caroline Craig

France celebrates the feast of Epiphany on the 6th of January with dessert – a Galette, a Gâteau or a Couronne des Rois to mark the arrival of the three kings in Bethlehem. A tiny porcelain figurine, known as the *fève*, is hidden inside the cake before it is baked. When the cake is cut, the youngest person in the room slides under the table and calls out the name of the person who should receive each slice, and whoever finds the fève becomes king or queen for the day.

In Provence, we opt for a Couronne des Rois over a galette. The lesser-known *couronne* (meaning crown) is an orange blossom-flavoured brioche, decorated with candied fruit and crunchy pearls of sugar. Its soft, light texture is most welcome after the indulgences of Christmas, and one I much prefer to the frangipane-filled puff pastry of the galette.

This couronne recipe is my great-aunt Edmée's. She will double or even quadruple the quantities, making multiple couronnes at a time to give away to friends and family. Is there anything lovelier than gifting someone a homemade cake? I once cycled the fifteen kilometres home from her house with one precariously tied to the back of my rickety bike.

Serves 8

For the couronne:
20g (¾oz) fresh yeast or 7g (¼oz) dried yeast
5 tbsp tepid milk, plus extra for brushing
300g (10½oz) plain flour, plus extra for dusting
Zest of 1 orange
1 tbsp orange blossom water
60g (2¼oz) caster sugar
2 eggs, lightly beaten
80g (2¾oz) butter, softened
40g (1½oz) chopped candied peel
1 porcelain fève (or whole almond)

For decoration:
3 tbsp apricot jam
1 tsp orange blossom water
8 candied fruit pieces
8 glacé cherries
2–3 tbsp pearl sugar

First activate the yeast: crumble or sprinkle into a bowl containing the milk. Mix in 50g (1¾oz) of the flour, then cover with a clean tea towel. Leave in a warm place for an hour or so, until the dough has risen a little and bubbles have formed: your 'starter' is now ready.

Grate the orange zest into a large mixing bowl containing the sugar and orange blossom water. Mix, then sift over the remaining flour. Add the beaten eggs, softened butter and prepared starter. Mix with a spoon, then take over with your hands. Knead for a few minutes. The dough will be quite sticky.

Transfer the dough to a clean surface sprinkled with flour and continue to knead for 15 minutes. If after 8 minutes the dough is still very sticky, add a little extra flour.

Shape the dough into a ball and put it back in the mixing bowl. Cover the bowl tightly with the tea towel and place in a draught-free, warm spot. Leave until the dough has doubled in size. This will take between 2 and 3 hours in a toasty place.

Once risen, depress the dough and allow the air to escape. Knead for a minute on a lightly floured surface, then roll into a circle about 2cm (¾in) thick. Transfer to a baking tray lined with baking paper. Stick a finger in the centre of your dough and make a hole, then move your finger around to increase the aperture so that you make a shape like a giant bagel with a central hole about 5cm (2in) in diameter.

Sprinkle the chopped candied peel on the dough immediately around the hole and nestle the fève or almond among it. Fold the outer edges of the dough inwards, over the candied fruit, and press to seal with the inner edge, forming a sort of giant stuffed bagel: your couronne.

Carefully flip the couronne upside down (the bottom side is generally prettier), then cover and prove once more in a warm place for 2 hours. Towards the end of the proving time, preheat the oven to 180°C/350°F/gas mark 4.

When you're ready to bake, brush the cake with a little milk. Bake for 15–20 minutes until the top is a lovely deep, golden colour.

Once out of the oven, decorate the couronne while it's still warm. Put the apricot jam in a small saucepan with the orange blossom water. Gently heat for a minute, then brush over the cake to glaze. Top with glacé cherries and candied fruit, followed by a generous sprinkling of pearl sugar.

A Menu for January

by Emiko Davies

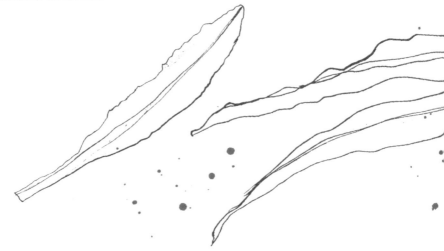

WINTER GREENS CROSTINI WITH BOTTARGA

In her 1954 cookbook *Italian Food*, Elizabeth David introduced her readers
to crostini as part of a hot antipasto in a way that still holds true today: 'These
little dishes are comforting in the cold weather, are good at lunch or supper and
facilitate life for the cook. But they should, I think, remain simple and small.
Enlarged to the size of hefty Welsh rarebits or club sandwiches, they lose their
point and their charm.' Simple is key. There is no need to take longer than
10 minutes to make crostini, and these, with garlicky winter greens such as
cavolo nero, are a perfect example. To add a bit of kick, you could toss some chilli
through the pan too, but I love this topped with just a light grating of bottarga
(cured fish roe), which adds such an unexpected, punchy flavour.

Makes 8 crostini

1 large bunch (about 1kg/2lb 4oz) cavolo nero
4 thick slices of crusty Italian bread, halved to give 8 pieces
(or 8 slices of baguette cut on a diagonal)
1 garlic clove, thinly sliced
3–4 tbsp extra virgin olive oil
Juice of ½ lemon
2 tsp grated bottarga
Sea salt and freshly ground black pepper

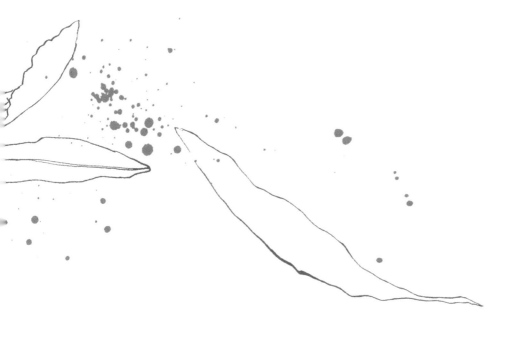

Cook the cavolo nero in boiling salted water for 4–5 minutes until tender, then plunge into ice-cold water to stop the cooking process. Pat dry with kitchen paper, remove the central vein, then chop roughly. You can do this ahead of time if needed, even the day before, and store in the fridge in an airtight container.

Toast the slices of bread on a griddle pan.

Meanwhile, put the garlic and about 2–3 tablespoons of the olive oil in a pan, place over a medium heat and gently cook the garlic until softened but not browned – essentially, you want to infuse the oil with the garlic. Add the blanched greens and toss for 1 minute or so until they are glossy, deep green and well coated in the garlicky oil. Add a good pinch of salt and pepper and squeeze over the lemon juice. Taste for seasoning (bearing in mind the bottarga is quite salty). Remove from the heat.

Drizzle the rest of the olive oil over the warm toasted crostini, top with the cavolo nero and grated bottarga, and serve immediately.

LENTIL AND SAUSAGE STEW

In central and northern Italy, it has long been considered good luck to eat lentils on New Year's Day. According to an old tradition, eating lentils, which are round and small like coins, will bring good fortune and money to the family in the new year. This is a versatile dish – you can make it more of a soup by keeping it brothy, or you can reduce it right down, almost like a legume version of sausages and mash.

Serves 6-8

300g (10½oz) dried brown lentils
3 tbsp olive oil
1 celery stick, finely chopped
1 medium carrot, finely chopped
1 medium onion, finely chopped
2 garlic cloves, finely chopped
200g (7oz) canned whole peeled tomatoes (about half a can)
125ml (4fl oz) dry white wine (or water)
2 bay leaves
1 small dried chilli, finely chopped (optional)
6–8 small pork and fennel sausages
Extra virgin olive oil, to serve
Sea salt and freshly ground black pepper

Rinse and drain the lentils and set aside.

Put the olive oil in a cast-iron casserole or similar pan, followed by the chopped celery, carrot, onion and garlic and a good pinch of salt. Cook gently over a low heat for about 15 minutes, stirring occasionally with a wooden spoon, until the vegetables are soft but not brown.

Add the tomatoes, breaking them up with the spoon, followed by the wine (or water). Increase the heat to medium–high and cook for 2–3 minutes. Add the lentils, bay leaves and chilli (if using), then cover with about 1.5 litres (2½ pints) of water. Season with salt and pepper and bring the mixture to a simmer.

Cover the casserole and reduce the heat right down to a slow simmer. Cook for about 1 hour, checking occasionally and topping up with water if it is reducing too quickly, then add the sausages, nestling them into the lentils, and cook for a further 20 minutes or so until cooked through and the lentils are tender.

Adjust the seasoning and ladle the stew into shallow bowls. Serve with a little drizzle of extra virgin olive oil.

Leftovers are delicious; when reheating, you may need to add some water to loosen the lentils.

SPICY BITTER ORANGE JAM WITH PECORINO CHEESE

Makes 4-5 jars

I love finishing a meal with a little platter of cheese while lingering over a glass of wine. Living in Florence, I discovered that cheese goes very well with something jammy, sweet and spicy all at once: *mostarda*, a north Italian condiment that's made with quince or pear and spiced with mustard essence – not for the faint of heart. But I've also been served delicious fig compotes, marmalades and chestnut honey alongside a cheese platter. It was while admiring the prolific bitter orange trees that line the terraced garden at the back of my butcher's shop that he suggested I take some fruit and try making a jam with a hint of chilli, which he thought would go well with pecorino cheese. He was right. The method is less fiddly than the usual one for British-style marmalade and it comes from a Sicilian way of making jam with citrus (lemons specifically), where, rather than chopping the peel so that it floats in a clear jelly, the flesh and rinds are passed through a *passaverdura* or mouli, resulting in a uniform purée.

1kg (2lb 4oz) bitter oranges
1.5kg (3lb 5oz) granulated sugar
5-6 small dried chillies, finely chopped
4 tbsp red wine vinegar

Wash the fruit carefully and cut off the little buttons on the tops where the fruit was attached to the stalk, then place the whole fruit in a large pot or preserving pan, covered with 2–2.5 litres (4½–5 pints) of water. Boil until the skins become incredibly soft – about 2 hours, or if they're small, 1 hour might be enough. Remove the oranges, reserving the cooking water and topping up, if necessary, so you have about 1.5 litres (3¾ pints) of liquid.

Cut the oranges into quarters and remove any seeds, then pass the fruit through a passaverdura or mouli set over a bowl (the brilliance of this contraption is that it will pass through the pulp and rind while sifting out unwanted bits such as the membranes, which need to be discarded). You should end up with a thick, smooth, pulpy mass. You can also do this with a blender, though to avoid the slightly bitter membranes you will first need to scoop out the flesh, scrape the pith and membranes from the rind (I use a spoon) and then put the cleaned flesh and rinds into the blender and blend.

Return this pulp to the pan with the reserved liquid, along with the sugar, chillies and vinegar.

Bring the jam to the boil over a high heat and boil rapidly for 20–30 minutes for a soft set. To test it, put a little saucer in the freezer, place a blob of hot marmalade on it, return it to the freezer for 30 seconds and then check it. Poke it or tilt the saucer a little: if the jam crinkles, it is ready. If it is too runny, keep boiling and checking every 5 minutes or so.

Leave the jam to cool for 10 minutes then ladle the hot jam into sterilised, dry jars. Seal the lids tightly (a tea towel helps protect your hands from the hot jars) and set aside. As the jam cools, the seals should tighten and contract – you'll hear a pop to confirm this. Store the jars somewhere cool and dry; once opened, store in the fridge.

Serve in little bowls next to a platter of pecorino cheese of different ages – young pecorino is mild, delicate and fresh, while aged pecorino is nuttier, darker and crumblier. If you can't find young pecorino, asiago could be a nice replacement, and a good, 36-month-old Parmesan could replace the aged pecorino.

Reading List

Michael Bond,
A Bear Called Paddington
A heartwarming and hilarious classic
about a very unusual bear who loves
marmalade sandwiches.

Jennifer McLagan,
Bitter
A fascinating exploration of bitter
flavours through science, history and
deliciously idiosyncratic recipes from the
champion of underappreciated foods.

Russell Norman,
Polpo
Simple recipes that capture the
unfrequented corners, bustling *bàcari*
and intricate waterways of Venice.
Try the Treviso risotto.

Anna Del Conte, *Amaretto,*
Apple Cake and Artichokes
Recipes and anecdotes from the
doyenne of Italian cooking, ranging
from the best way to make a tomato
sauce to a menu for a sumptuous
Renaissance dinner.

Rachel de Thample,
Tonics & Teas
A charming collection of traditional
remedies to soothe and comfort,
from kombucha, kefir and medicinal
vinegars to tonics such as elderberry
syrup with echinacea and ginger.

Caroline Craig,
Provence
Escape to the sun-drenched foothills
of the French Mediterranean and
discover how to cook and eat the
Provençal way. Bake the chocolate
orange gâteau after you've perfected
your *couronne des rois*.

Emiko Davies,
Tortellini at Midnight
Heirloom recipes from Taranto to
Turin to Tuscany. Take inspiration
from the family tradition of ringing in
the new year with *tortellini al sugo* and
a glass of *spumante*.

February

Dark mornings and weary spirits call for the comfort of British classics and the thrill of bland food. Brave brassicas, sturdy winter greens and the neon-pink glow of forced rhubarb provide a welcome balance to rib-sticking pies, hearty soups and puddings drenched in custard – slow, gentle cooking for slow, gentle days.

IN SEASON

Bittercress
Chicory
Flower sprouts
Forced rhubarb
Mandarins

Pink grapefruit
Primroses
Puntarelle
Savoy cabbage
Sprouting broccoli

Sprouting Broccoli

BRAVE BRASSICAS

The monotony of dark winter days is pierced by the first spears of sprouting broccoli arriving at the market – elegant long stems with tight flower buds in hues of green, white and purple, picked before they open into bright yellow flowers. Like all brassicas, they brave the cold, standing strong against the hardest frosts.

Sprouting broccoli may be tough in the ground, but it needs a tender touch in the kitchen. Pamper it as you would the first bunches of asparagus, trimming only the very ends of the stems and steaming the tips just above the water. The florets are easily damaged, especially on the more delicate white-sprouting, so cook *al dente*, retaining a pleasant firmness when you bite.

Brassicas get a bad rap in British cooking – a sordid history of over-boiled cabbage and soggy Brussels sprouts – yet the Italians aren't afraid of cooking broccoli twice: first boiling it to a delicious mush, then dragging it around a pan in a glossy pool of olive oil infused with garlic and chilli, purposefully breaking it down so it coats each strand of pasta. Anchovy is a good addition to this *broccoli ripassati* (as anchovy often is) and leftovers are excellent on toast.

Sprouting broccoli isn't fussy about what it shares a plate with: drench it in cream and roast it in a gratin; add to a frittata with chorizo or ricotta; stir-fry with garlic, ginger and soy; or grill until charred and blistered to serve alongside salmon or slow-braised pork belly. It can stand alone too, needing no accompaniment except a spoonful of sauce, such as maltaise, a hollandaise spiked with the juice and zest of blood oranges. Graced with an egg, scrambled or fried, the tender spears make a satisfying lunch, a favourite recipe with the English since the early eighteenth century, according to Jane Grigson. Just make sure you have your plate warmed in readiness – sprouting broccoli is impatient and quick to go cold.

A NEW ARRIVAL

Flower sprouts, or kalettes as they are now branded, are a modern invention – a cross between Brussels sprouts and kale – and are sweeter than other brassicas. These tiny rosettes look rather fetching with their ruffled green leaves flecked with purple. Try them briefly boiled and dressed with anchovies and melted butter pepped up with garlic and lemon zest. Perfect next to grilled lamb cutlets, smoked haddock or by the side of your favourite stew or fish pie.

Palest Greens
by Amy Key

```
I dreamed a recipe:
peelings from a pear
and the hard stem
of broccoli,
dressed in lime juice
and olive oil.
I called this recipe
Palest Greens.
It was February
and I was craving.
Not that kind.
```

MAKE AHEAD

Pickled rhubarb

A jar of neon-pink forced rhubarb will brighten the dreariest day, positively glowing at the back of the fridge. Add chillies and slices of fresh ginger to the pickling brine for a little heat, or try orange peel, pink peppercorns and star anise. Irresistible paired with oily fish, cured meats and cheese, it also works brilliantly chopped through salads and salsas. Keep the vinegar for dressings, shrubs and spritely cocktails.

Siberian Railroad Picnicking

by Caroline Eden

'Potato?' asked Andrei, my cabin-mate, as he passed me a mud-coloured orb. The 'potato' was, in fact, a chocolate ball given to him by his mother on the platform of Irkutsk railway station as he boarded the train. Taking the 'potato', I offered a handful of dried apricots in return.

Travelling second-class on the Trans-Siberian Railway, stretching 5,772 miles from Moscow to Vladivostok on the Pacific edge of Asia, meant seven days in a four-berth compartment and a constant flow of different passengers. Rarely moving faster than 43 miles per hour, there was ample time to swap tales, and food. Crucially, this camaraderie fosters a sense of togetherness – reassuring, given that the environment outside is truly forbidding. The station names reflect the scenery: there is Zima ('winter' in Russian), and Kuytun ('cold' in the language of the Buryat people).

Only by travelling the rails, the *zhelyeznaya doroga* or 'iron road', can you really appreciate the enormity of the largest country on earth. Flying back to Moscow from my final stop would take nine hours. I gazed out of the window, hypnotised by small settlements of picket-fenced *dachas* (summer houses) and Siberian log huts with painted shutters, clustered together by the railway tracks as if cowering from the snow. Women on station platforms braved blizzards and temperatures of almost 30°C below zero (−22°F) to sell furs, knitted socks and russet-coloured dried fish. The trip was a chance to escape, to recuperate. A holiday, of sorts. And everything, back then in 2016, seen from the window fascinated me.

Andrei and I stretched out on our bunks, watching the little television above our door that blared out a 1970s Soviet science-fiction film. Below us, under the fold-down bunks, heaters blasted hot air. As the train ploughed on through a whiteout, a curious smell began to hum. A bit like kipper, but stronger. I asked Andrei what it was. 'Omul', came the answer: a smoked oily fish sold in supermarkets and restaurants at Lake Baikal, not far from Irkutsk. Omul is wildly popular and our fellow Trans-Sibers were luxuriating in picnic feasts of it, radiators permeating the smell through the carriages.

A knock at the door announced the cheery entrance of our matronly *provodnitsa* (conductress). She'd come not to check tickets this time but to sell us *pirozhki*, little stuffed buns. I bought a cabbage one, thrilling in its blandness, and passed another across to Andrei.

Once the taiga began glowing a fiery sunset orange, I knew it was dinnertime. To get to the dining car, I darted through the freezing gaps that connect the carriages, following the smell of fried potatoes. *Solyanka* was on the menu, a briny sour soup with salty cured meats, olives and dill. To go with it, I chose cold Baltika beer. Spooning the soup, I pushed back the frilly yellow curtains and watched timber mills and gingerbread houses rush past. The cook, dressed in a leopard-print tracksuit, appeared momentarily, greeting me with a wink, her tangerine hair artfully curled in a mohican of pink plastic rollers.

Outside, a frozen river shone, but a belching coal factory on the embankment quickly killed any romantic ideas about ice fishing. Then, a giant prison, surrounded by watchtowers and barbed wire. I considered the fact that I had another two nights without showering to go and wondered whose vodka-laced breath would fill the coupé next. But as I drained my beer, watching the glittering snowy forests disappear into the gloaming, I found myself content – happy, even.

Solyanka
by Darra Goldstein

Brined pickles and lemon slices give this hearty Russian soup a wonderfully sour tang. *Solyanka* can be made with meat or fish, but it always contains a generous mix of ingredients. I make the standard meat-based soup a bit more elegant by adding veal, but feel free to substitute chicken – or grouse, as nineteenth-century Russians liked to do. You can find pickled mushrooms online or make some yourself.

Serves 4–6

1.14kg (2½lb) braising steak, with bones
1.5 litres (2¾ pints) water
About 1 tsp salt, to taste
60g (2¼oz) unsalted butter
2 onions, peeled and chopped
450g (1lb) stewing veal, cut into 2.5cm (1in) cubes
2 tbsp plain flour
1 large garlic clove, crushed
115g (4oz) smoked ham, cut into 2.5cm (1in) cubes
115g (4oz) frankfurters, cut into 6mm (¼in) slices
400g (14oz) can of tomatoes, drained and coarsely chopped
1 tsp tomato purée
2 medium pickled cucumbers, julienned
70g (2½oz) black olives, such as Kalamata, pitted and halved
1 tbsp capers
115g (4oz) pickled mushrooms, drained
1 bay leaf
2 lemon slices, 2.5cm (1in) thick
Freshly ground black pepper, to taste
Soured cream, to serve (optional)

Put the braising steak in a large stockpot with the water. Cover and bring to a boil, skimming off any froth that rises to the surface. Reduce the heat to very low and simmer, covered, for 1½ hours. Using a slotted spoon, remove the meat from the pot, separate it from the bone, and weigh out 225g (8oz), reserving any extra for another use. Cut the meat into 2.5cm (1in) pieces and sprinkle with ½ teaspoon of the salt and plenty of freshly ground pepper. Return the pieces of salted meat to the stockpot with the broth.

Melt half the butter in a large frying pan and add the onions. Cook over a medium-low heat, stirring occasionally, until the onions are softened and starting to brown.

Meanwhile, sprinkle the veal with the remaining salt, add pepper to taste, then dredge it in the flour. When the onions are ready, move them to the side of the pan and add the remaining butter. Increase the heat slightly and cook the veal, stirring occasionally, until it is lightly browned on both sides – about 4–5 minutes.

Stir in the garlic, ham and frankfurters, mixing everything well, and cook for 1–2 minutes. Then tip this meat and onion mixture into the stockpot. Cover and simmer for 15 minutes. Stir in the tomatoes, tomato purée, pickled cucumbers, olives, capers, mushrooms, bay leaf and lemon slices and simmer for a further 10 minutes.

Serve with a dollop of soured cream, if desired.

My Victorian Appetite

by Alexander Lobrano

When my London-bound 747 lumbered down the runway in New York on a sparkling September morning in 1976, little did I know I was soon to become a student of not only Thomas Hardy and William Morris as planned, but of pie and beans, jellied eels and treacle tart. My decision to study abroad was born of an obsessive fascination with Victorian Britain; its literature, art, architecture and engineering – especially the massive steel-girder railway viaducts leading into the grand neo-Gothic stations of cities like Glasgow and Birmingham. With no premeditation, but somewhat inevitably, I also became an avid pupil of the cooking and foods that had nourished the Victorian builders.

What I immediately discovered when I arrived in London was that a newspaper cone of fish and chips or a good fry-up in a greasy spoon not only moved me in ways Robert Browning never would, but that these foods created a potent personal intimacy with a period of time and a way of life I'd never known. Alluringly salty, fatty, crispy, savoury and sour, the diet that sustained the Victorian working class was easy to love. It was cheap, comforting, humble and easily shared.

Responding to an ad in *Time Out*, I ended up sharing a room with a lovely Australian in an unheated maisonette in Fulham Broadway. Since I had no money, I lived in a way that was a world removed from my affluent, emotionally chilly upbringing in leafy and somewhat smug suburban Connecticut. I was broke, shy, educated and American, and so a total puzzle to the people who casually populated my daily life in Fulham. Why, wondered Dimitrios, the Cypriot barber who ran the shop below our maisonette, would anyone willingly forsake all of those casual American comforts seen on television – central heating, kitchens with huge fridges, dishwashers and so on?

Always quick with a saucy remark, the kind ladies of the North End Road Market gave me broken carrots and bruised potatoes when they broke down their stands, plus the occasional bosomy hug or pinch on the cheek, while the maiden librarians at the large red-brick public library made me misty-eyed when they invited me to their staff party. They sent me home – woozy from too much Harvey's Bristol Cream – with a tartan carrier bag filled with homemade pies and a tin of frosted biscuits, which, when I opened it, smelled softly of bedsit, or talcum powder and sour milk.

The neighbourhood heaved with simple restaurants serving scampi and chips, jellied eels and mash, egg-bacon-chips, beans on toast, or steak and kidney pie,

but my favourite was the one with frilly white nylon curtains. The pink Formica tables had a Sputnik pattern and were perpetually damp (the rapid turnover of customers was such that they had always just been wiped clean). There was a waitress called Tracey, who was constantly telling people that the curtains were made from her old knickers and that she was an old tart and proud of it. Without calling any attention to it, they actually baked their own bread every day and made delicious cakes. Their black pudding, also homemade, was excellent. And, because the owner was Anglo-Italian, the spaghetti bolognese was light years from the overcooked pasta in sweet tomato sauce usually found in such places.

I lived in London for a second time after finishing university and, the enduring appeal of Bird's custard, Branston pickle and Marmite notwithstanding, the British diet had already started to change during Thatcher's years. To wit, it was a lot less British. The once-pervasive smell of frying, especially with suet, was missing. Then the microwave oven upended everything by ushering in ready meals that stirred pleasant memories of holidays in Mediterranean countries. Today, of course, you can still find pies of various kinds in British supermarkets, along with Cornish pasties, Scotch eggs and Cumberland sausages, but jellied eels and mash has become a sort of arty heritage food.

For my part, even though I've lived in Paris for many years, I still miss the sweetness, sincerity and even the food of the tearooms and caffs that nourished me as a student. And I often think of those meals when, despite my French partner's theatrical revulsion, I occasionally treat myself to beans on toast on a gusty night in Gaul.

A Menu for February
by Calum Franklin

CHICORY, PEAR AND BLUE CHEESE SALAD

My favourite salads are often the simplest – just a few ingredients that work well as a team. Here, a cooling blue cheese dressing counterbalances the crisp, slightly bitter chicory, rounded off with just a little sweetness from the pear.

```
Serves 4

100g (3½oz) blue cheese
1 tbsp white wine vinegar
Juice of ½ lemon
100g (3½oz) mayonnaise
50ml (2fl oz) soured cream
20g (¾oz) walnut halves
2 heads white chicory
4 heads red chicory
2 Conference pears
```

Cut the blue cheese in half and put one wedge in the freezer for at least 3 hours. Whisk the vinegar and lemon juice with the mayonnaise and soured cream. Crumble in the remaining blue cheese, mix well and set aside.

Spread the walnuts on a baking sheet and toast at 180°C/350°F/gas mark 4 for 5 minutes. Remove and allow to cool.

Prepare the chicory by slicing through the base (discarding the stems) to separate the leaves, then transfer to a large mixing bowl. Quarter and core the unpeeled pear and slice thinly. Add to the chicory.

Liberally dress the leaves and pear in the blue cheese dressing and pile onto a large serving platter. Spoon any remaining dressing over the top.

Remove the frozen blue cheese from the freezer and grate finely all over the salad. Crumble the toasted walnuts over the top of the salad and serve.

BEEF, CELERIAC AND PINK FIR POTATO PIE

A pie in February should be a comforting affair and here the beef, celeriac
and potato are your slippers, blanket and sofa, the suet pastry your wood fire.

Serves 4–6

For the filling:
600g (1lb 5oz) beef chuck steak
100g (3½oz) plain flour
3 tbsp rapeseed oil
3 Spanish onions, thinly sliced
500g (1lb 2oz) Pink Fir potatoes, halved
200ml (7fl oz) red wine
1 bay leaf
2 litres (4¼ pints) beef stock
3 rosemary sprigs, leaves picked and finely chopped
1 celeriac, peeled and roughly diced
1 egg yolk, beaten with 1 tsp water
Sea salt and freshly ground black pepper

For the pastry:
275g (9¾oz) self-raising flour
1 tsp salt
100g (3½oz) shredded suet, frozen
75g (2¾oz) butter, frozen
125ml (4fl oz) ice-cold water

Preheat the oven to 220°C/425°F/gas mark 7. In a large roasting tray, mix
the beef with the plain flour until fully absorbed, then add half of the oil and
coat well. Roast the beef for 20–30 minutes until browned and any juices have
evaporated.

Meanwhile, heat the remaining oil in a large saucepan over a medium heat and
add the onions. Cook until just starting to brown, then add the potatoes, red wine
and bay leaf and gently cook until the wine has reduced by half. Next add the
stock, rosemary and 1 teaspoon of salt and bring up to a simmer.

When the meat is ready, pour the onion and potato mixture directly into the roasting
tray and add the diced celeriac. Gently move the beef around with a wooden spoon
to dislodge it from the base, then tightly cover the tray with foil. Return to the oven,
reduce the heat to 160°C/325°F/gas mark 3 and cook for 2 hours.

Just before the end of the cooking time, start to make the pastry. Put the flour
and salt into a large bowl and add the frozen suet. Grate in the frozen butter and

stir together with a fork until well coated with flour. Pour in the cold water and gently mix together until a dough starts to form. Transfer to a clean work surface and lightly knead without overworking. Shape into a rough rectangle, cover and place in the fridge to rest for at least 20 minutes.

Remove the beef from the oven and strain the liquid through a colander into a pan. Transfer the strained beef and vegetables to a bowl and place the pan of liquid over a medium heat to reduce until thick enough to coat the back of a wooden spoon. When the required consistency is reached, check the seasoning and add lots of freshly ground black pepper. Pour the liquid back over the beef mixture and allow to cool to room temperature.

Remove the dough from the fridge and roll out to a large rectangle 5mm (¼in) thick. It should be large enough to cover a 25 x 18cm (10 x 7in) pie dish, with an extra 2cm (¾in) overhang all the way round. Put the pastry onto a large baking tray lined with baking paper and pop it back into the fridge for 10 minutes. Increase the oven temperature to 200°C/400°F/gas mark 6.

Transfer the cooled filling to the pie dish and brush the rim of the dish 2.5cm (1in) down the outside with a little of the egg yolk. Remove the pastry from the fridge and lay it over the filling. Press the overlap onto the brushed sides of the pie dish and trim a little if necessary.

Brush the pastry top with the remaining egg yolk and put the pie in the oven for 30 minutes. Serve with green vegetables – I love this pie with cavolo nero.

BRAEBURN EVE'S PUDDING WITH CALVADOS CUSTARD

As a child, this pudding would often end our family Sunday lunch and I adore it still. It's a celebration of two things we do very well in the UK: apple growing and Victoria sponge. Warming the custard with a touch of Calvados is an adult indulgence but always welcome.

```
Serves 4

1 vanilla pod, halved
500g (1lb 2oz) Braeburn apples, peeled, cored and roughly diced
115g (4oz) salted butter, softened
115g (4oz) caster sugar
2 large eggs, beaten
115g (4oz) self-raising flour

For the custard:
150ml (5fl oz) whole milk
150ml (5fl oz) double cream
3 large egg yolks
25g (1oz) caster sugar
50ml (2fl oz) Calvados or cider brandy
```

Preheat the oven to 180°C/350°F/gas mark 4.

Put 3 tablespoons of water into a saucepan. Scrape the seeds from half the vanilla pod (keep the other half for the custard) into the water then add the pod itself. Add the apples, bring to a simmer and cook for 3 minutes. Transfer to an ovenproof dish big enough for the apples to cover the bottom.

In a mixing bowl whisk the butter and sugar together until pale and fluffy, then add the eggs, a little at a time, whisking after each addition until combined. Fold in the flour.

Spread the batter evenly over the apples and bake for 30 minutes.

Meanwhile, make the custard. Beat the eggs and sugar together in a bowl until combined. Put the milk, cream and remaining vanilla in a saucepan over a medium heat until just beginning to simmer. Remove the vanilla pod and discard. Pour the hot liquid over the sugar and eggs whisking continuously until well combined. Pour back into the pan and cook gently over a medium heat until thickened. Remove from the heat and whisk in the Calvados.

Serve the pudding straight from the oven with the hot custard in a jug.

Reading List

Laura B. Russell,
Brassicas
Inventive recipes that celebrate the intrinsic flavours of brassicas instead of masking them under layers of cheese or boiling them to death.

Nigel Slater,
Tender: Volume I
A comprehensive and deeply personal guide to growing and cooking vegetables, told with wit, enthusiasm and a charming lack of pretension. The extensive gardening notes will prove useful for veg patches and allotments.

Caroline Eden,
Red Sands
A passport to the food, forgotten histories and landscapes of Central Asia, from the shores of the Caspian Sea to the remote orchards of Tajikistan.

Darra Goldstein,
Beyond the North Wind
Recipes and lore from the wild northern corners of Russia. Try the soured cream honey cake and the pepper vodka.

Alexander Lobrano,
My Place at the Table
A moving memoir, a testament to the healing power of food, and a recipe for a delicious life in Paris.

Edwin Heathcote,
London Caffs
An affectionate look at the fast-disappearing caffs of London, illustrated with architectural photographs documenting the Formica tables and gleaming chrome machines that have produced 'frothy coffee' and huge quantities of tea since the 1940s.

Calum Franklin,
The Pie Room
A masterclass in pastry from the chef responsible for reviving one of the very best British culinary contributions. The cheesy dauphinoise and caramelised onion pie is a must.

March

The hope of spring bursts forth in March – fresh green shoots forcing their way through the cold, hard ground. Go for bracing walks and feel the surge of energy beneath your feet, returning with satisfying bags of wild spring greens. The chill and rain may linger, but spirits begin to lift, especially when the cupboards are full and there are feasts to plan and cook.

IN SEASON

Babington's leek	Nettles
Birch sap	Sea kale
Chickweed	Spring greens
Dandelion leaves	Spring onions
Magnolia flowers	Wild garlic

Spring Onions

Spring onions once belonged to their season, appearing among the first green shoots of spring. Like other alliums, they are the most underrated of vegetables, often relegated to mere garnish. Yet these elegant onions are endlessly useful and should be celebrated alongside more conspicuous seasonal ingredients.

Essentially immature onions, harvested before the bulb has had a chance to swell, spring onions can in fact be grown from many varieties. Look for slender long tops that are stiff and dark green, and firm bulbs with the roots intact. Used raw, spring onions add a welcome freshness to everything from salsas to egg mayo sandwiches. Show them off in an English garden salad dressed with homemade salad cream – a classic in need of a revival. To mellow the familiar onion tang, cut the leaves lengthways into fine strips and drop them into cold water – they will lose some of their pungency and tighten into attractive curls.

Spring onions are used to their full advantage across Asia. Sizzled in a wok with garlic and ginger, stir-fried whole as a vegetable, and scattered over a finished dish, they act as both backbone ingredient and seasoning. They are essential in Chinese *Cong you bing* or Korean *Pajeon* – spring onion pancakes served with a dipping sauce – and they sizzle in the ginger and spring onion oil poured over Hainanese chicken rice.

Closer to home, they feature in traditional Irish champ – also charmingly known as cally, pandy, poundies and stelk – the comforting dish of spring onions cooked in milk and whipped into mashed potato to form a creamy fluff. A substantial lump of butter should be dropped into the middle of each mound so you can eat the mash methodically from the outside in, dipping it into the melted pool.

The plumpest bulbs can be cooked whole, grilled and dressed with a splash of balsamic vinegar, or thrown on hot coals to take on a deep smoky flavour. Chop them through a salsa verde or pair with steak and bernaise. Cooked in this way, spring onions are reminiscent of Spanish calçots, barbecued over fire and dipped into *romesco* or *salbitxada* once the charred outer layer has been peeled away. Calçotada festivals are held all over Catalonia from January to April – celebratory feasts to take inspiration from when the first green shoots appear.

KNOW YOUR ALLIUMS

Look for three-cornered leeks when out foraging for wild greens – easy to spot with their tiny white flowers and unique triangular stems. If you're close to the sea, forage for Babington's leek. Native only to Britain, the Channel Islands and Ireland, their mild and slightly garlicky flavour is delicious in a spring vegetable tart.

MAKE AHEAD

Magnolia syrup

The spectacular flowers of the magnolia tree are among the first to bloom in spring. Both their delicate ginger-cardamom flavour and pale pink hue can be captured in sugar by simmering the petals in a simple syrup and leaving to steep overnight. Add a dash to something sparkling for a refreshing drink, drizzle on pancakes, or pour over ice cream when the weather warms.

Underrated Alliums

by Gill Meller

There are a handful of ingredients that are so familiar, I don't notice them anymore. Onions and garlic are two such ingredients. They store beautifully, which means they tend to be available all year round, so I don't look forward to cooking them in the way I might, say, new potatoes, elderflowers or gooseberries. These alliums are a mainstay in my kitchen, a constant. I use them habitually, as I do salt or fat. They form the foundations to countless recipes, their goodness is immeasurable, but once things are underway, they are all too often lost in the shadows of a dish.

I've settled into a routine with onions and garlic. I take up my tools automatically. I set the onions on my chopping board and use a sharp cook's knife – onions are very good at telling you if your knife is sharp – to split each one in half. The halves get peeled, inconsiderately, then sliced from root to tip. I place a large, heavy pan over a medium-high heat and pour in a little puddle of peppery olive oil. When I can see the surface of the oil move, I drop in the butter. It sounds angry, until it succumbs. I scrape the sliced onion off my board into the bubbling butter – the onion screams! – and reach for a wooden spoon to settle things down.

There's a white bowl full of garlic by the stove. I bash a bulb with my hand, but it's never as easy as we all make out. Eventually, the cloves part. I use the tip of my knife to nick off the pointy ends, and if I turn the bulb at the same time, the skin usually comes off too. I nearly always slice my garlic. Occasionally, I'll do it carefully, so it's paper thin, but most of the time, I don't even look down. If it's getting cooked gently for several hours, it doesn't matter how finely it's sliced. The garlic joins the onions and I add a few pinches of sea salt and crack in some black pepper. I stir them together, I see the steam rise, I judge the pitch and tone of the sizzling, and I adjust the heat.

This is how things begin and it all happens without me really thinking. Half the time, I could be somewhere else entirely. At least, that's how it used to be.

Last year I created my own little vegetable garden to grow some of the food I love to eat. I planted all sorts of things, including onions and garlic. Preparing homegrown onions and garlic is incredibly rewarding. In fact, it's blown my mind. Growing my own has helped me notice these two wonderful ingredients again; it's helped me realise how special they are, and how much time and effort goes into producing them. Now when I'm chopping onions or slicing garlic, I'm looking and I'm actually seeing. I don't want to lose them anymore; I want to venerate them, I want to taste them.

ONION TART

```
1 tbsp extra virgin olive oil
A large knob of unsalted butter
8 large onions, halved and thinly sliced
4 thyme sprigs, leaves picked
2 bay leaves
4 garlic cloves, thinly sliced
2 tbsp soft light brown sugar
2 tbsp red wine vinegar
1 tbsp Dijon mustard
320g shortcrust pastry, chilled
Flaky sea salt and freshly ground black pepper
```

Heat the oil in a large, heavy-based pan over a medium heat, then add the butter. Once it is bubbling, add the onions, thyme and bay leaves and season with plenty of salt and pepper. Reduce the heat a little and stir the onions regularly for 10–12 minutes until they are beginning to soften. Then, place a lid on the pan and cook for 1 hour, stirring every so often, until the onions have reduced to a thick, sweet compote of sorts.

Remove the lid from the pan, make a little clearing in the onions and add the garlic. Sizzle it lightly, then fold it into the onions, along with the sugar and vinegar. Stir well. Cook for a further 20–25 minutes, or until the onions are dark, thick, heartbreakingly soft, and just beginning to catch on the base of the pan. Stir in the mustard, taste and adjust the seasoning if necessary. Remove the pan from the heat and allow the onions to cool a little while you make the tart case.

Preheat the oven to 180°C/350°F/gas mark 4.

Roll out the chilled dough into a thin circle large enough to line a fluted 24-cm (9½-in) loose-bottomed tart tin, leaving an overhang. Prick the base, then line it with baking paper and baking beans. Blind-bake for 20 minutes, then remove the paper and beans and return the case to the oven for a further 5 minutes, or until the base is dry and lightly coloured. Remove from the oven and trim the overhang. Carefully scrape the onion mixture into the tart case and use a spoon to level off.

Bake the tart for 15–20 minutes, until the onion filling is just firm to the touch and a lovely dark colour. Allow to cool a little before sprinkling with flaky sea salt and slicing.

Wine Snacks

by Fiona Beckett

March is not only the start of the hungry gap – the time of year when it seems there will never be anything to cook but root vegetables – but also the inspiration gap. One option is to abandon any pretence of being creative and fall back on your favourite foods, preferably in snack form – raising the bar, not so much with elaborate cooking but with the quality and ingenuity of your wine pairing. I appreciate that for us Brits there is nothing more comforting than a cuppa, but after months of winter, even that might be palling, so instead enliven your evening with one of these wine-snack combinations.

SAUCISSON AND BEAUJOLAIS

Beaujolais is still afflicted by its bubblegummy 'nouveau' image, but a good Beaujolais-Villages or a named *cru*, like Brouilly, is a joyous drink – a real *vin de soif*, as the French call it. And what better to nibble with it than a few slices of saucisson or salami? Instant picnic.

CHEESE TOASTIES AND CHARDONNAY

You *can* drink red wine with your toastie – 'course you can – but don't automatically assume it's the only option. *White* wine works really well with cheese. In the case of Cheddar, which is what most of us have in the fridge, make it a light, creamy chardonnay.

SUSHI AND PINOT GRIGIO

Like beaujolais, pinot grigio suffers from a reputational problem. Yet it's the very neutrality of this wine – and other crisp dry whites, including muscadet, picpoul de pinet and albariño – that preserves the subtle, delicate flavours of the raw fish and rice. That said, you'll benefit from paying a bit more for a pinot grigio from the mountainous region of Trentino-Alto Adige.

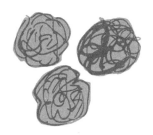

PAKORAS AND RIESLING

Wine is a far from traditional choice with Indian street foods like pakoras and bhajis, but, as with most spicy foods, these snacks benefit from a touch of sweetness in any accompanying drink. Step forward unloved riesling, which deserves its place in the sun. I particularly like those from Washington State.

CHIPS AND CHAMPAGNE

Frankly, champagne is great with anything deep-fried, but there's something particularly decadent about enjoying a bottle (or half bottle) with some crisp homemade chips – and a pot of mayo on the side for dunking, of course.

FRUIT CAKE AND MADEIRA

Madeira is a great addition to sauces and gravies, but it's also an excellent drink in its own right, especially with a good fruitcake. You could even add a dash to the cake when you make it. Sweet marsala works too.

CHOCOLATE BROWNIES, ICE CREAM AND PX SHERRY

Pedro ximenez is the most luxuriantly treacly of all sherries. Frequently paired with vanilla ice cream (which is pretty good – don't get me wrong) it is elevated to an even higher plane with a freshly baked brownie, a scoop of ice cream melting invitingly on top.

Nowruz

by Durkhanai Ayubi

For those whose lives follow the trajectory of displacement, food can form a powerful and meaningful way to reclaim and explore elements of identity otherwise lost. In 1985, when I was one, my family fled a war-torn Afghanistan, and by the time I was two, we had settled in Australia. A vast ocean away from our homeland, as my sisters and I grew up, food became a remedy to this schism in our family story. We drew upon the healing power of the rituals and cultural expressions embedded within Afghan cuisine as a way to stay tethered to our ancestral identity while unfolding into the expanse of the next chapter of our story.

One such formative and revelatory food memory arose every year in March during the celebration of Nowruz, the Afghan New Year, when we prepared a feast of symbolic dishes to mark the occasion – a tradition that endures in my family to this day.

Celebrated as one of the most important events in the calendar in countries crossed by the ancient Silk Roads – Iran, the Kurdish regions of Turkey, Iraq, Syria, India, throughout Central Asia – and in diaspora communities globally, Nowruz heralds in the new year in unison with the spring equinox. With its roots in ancient Zoroastrianism, the day has been commemorated for more than 3,000 years, marking the beginning of spring and celebrating the renewal of nature.

The food rituals associated with Nowruz reiterate this theme of new life. Dishes often include green ingredients, to capture the imagery of renewal – a spinach dish, *sabzi*, is always part of the Nowruz spread, along with a pudding called *samanak*, prepared using the newly germinated shoots of wheat. And, as an expression of the sweetness and joy that people wish one another for the year ahead, we make *haft mewa*, which translates as 'seven fruits'.

Haft mewa is a mix of dried fruits and nuts steeped in water until their flavours and natural sugars emerge and combine. Like most Afghan cuisine, it is best prepared collectively with family and friends. I still remember, as a child, sitting around the table with my sisters, laughing as we determinedly met the challenge of peeling walnuts, our will as stubborn as the skins clinging to the nuts.

All these years later, I realise something deeper was fermenting. Despite the erasures and all that is hollowed out about Afghanistan and its people, so many of whom are in various states of exile, staying close to the beauty of Afghan cuisine and the rituals surrounding it, has allowed me to grasp the depth and breadth of my story – to reclaim my heritage.

HAFT MEWA

Prepare this dish two days ahead of time to allow the flavours to develop. The recipe is flexible enough to add or omit particular ingredients according to personal taste. Sour apricots and *sinjid* (dried olives) can be found in Afghan and Iranian food shops.

Serves 6

100g (3½oz) almonds
100g (3½oz) walnuts
100g (3½oz) shelled pistachio nuts
300g (10½oz) sultanas
100g (3½oz) raisins
100g (3½oz) whole dried apricots
100g (3½oz) whole dried sour apricots, stone in
100g (3½oz) sinjid (dried Russian or Persian olives)
3 litres (6 ⅓ pints) boiling water

Soak each variety of nut separately in bowls of hot water for at least 30 minutes to help with removing the skins. Once the skins are slightly softened, drain the nuts and use your fingers to rub off the skins, dropping the skinned nuts into a very large heatproof container with a lid.

Add all the dried fruits to the nuts and mix well, then pour in the boiling water, place the lid on top and set aside to cool. Refrigerate for two days to allow the flavours to fully develop.

Serve chilled, ladling some syrup into each bowl. The haft mewa will keep in an airtight container in the fridge for up to a week.

A Menu for March
by Uyen Luu

WILD GARLIC AND PRAWN NOODLES

The ingredients for this simple Vietnamese recipe can be prepped ahead and require only a quick stir-fry, giving you plenty of time to be with your guests. These noodles offer warmth, freshness, lightness – all things that describe the start of spring. If you can't get wild garlic or garlic chives, use extra garlic or spring onions, or substitute coriander or Thai basil leaves. For less heat, simply reduce the amount of chilli, or omit it entirely.

Serves 4

½ tbsp ghee
4 garlic cloves, sliced
1–2 bird's eye chillies, finely chopped
8 king prawns, heads and shells on, washed and deveined
50g (1¾oz) glass noodles, soaked in cold water for 10 minutes then drained
50g (1¾oz) spring onions, thinly sliced lengthways
30g (1oz) wild garlic or garlic chives, roughly chopped
100ml (3½fl oz) aloe vera juice or coconut water
1 tbsp fish sauce

To serve:
Juice of ½ lime
Pinch of freshly ground black pepper
1 tbsp crispy chilli oil (optional)

Prepare all the ingredients before you start to cook. Heat a large frying pan over a high heat, then add the ghee, garlic and chillies and fry until the garlic starts to turn golden. Throw in the prawns and leave to sizzle for 1 minute, or until the bottoms have turned opaque and orange-pink, before adding the drained noodles, spring onions and wild garlic. Toss together for a further minute, then add the aloe vera juice or coconut water along with the fish sauce and stir-fry to combine. If it looks too dry, add another splash of aloe vera juice or coconut water. Once the greens have wilted and are embracing the noodles, remove from the heat and serve immediately on a large sharing plate with a good squeeze of lime, some black pepper and a kiss of crispy chilli oil.

LEMON SOLE WITH PASSION FRUIT AND GARLICKY SPRING GREENS

I love small gatherings – sharing food family-style around the table, wine glasses clinking, laughter and special tales being told with hopes of warmer and brighter times ahead. This unusual combination is one I like to serve on such occasions; all you need is steamed rice on the side.

Serves 4

1 tbsp rapeseed or vegetable oil
2 whole lemon sole (about 500g/1lb 2oz each) or 4 fillets
75g (2¾oz) spring greens, sliced into 1cm ribbons
150g (5½oz) trimmed purple sprouting broccoli, cut on the diagonal
into 10cm (4in) lengths
1 tsp ghee
3 garlic cloves, sliced
Sea salt and freshly ground black pepper

For the dressing:
2 garlic cloves
1 bird's eye chilli
Juice from ¼ lemon or lime
1 passion fruit
10g (¼oz) coriander stalks, sliced into 5mm (¼in) lengths
2 tbsp fish sauce

First, make the dressing using a pestle and mortar. Bash together the garlic, chilli and citrus juice until combined. Stir in the juice and seeds of the passion fruit, along with the coriander stalks and fish sauce. Set aside.

Heat the oil in a large frying pan over a medium heat and add the fish (if your pan cannot accommodate all the fish, fry one at a time). Season with a little salt and pepper and cook the whole fish for about 8 minutes on each side, or until golden and crispy (about 4 minutes if using fillets).

Meanwhile, bring a pan of water to the boil and gently poach the spring greens and purple sprouting for 3–4 minutes. Drain and leave in the colander. Using the same pan, heat the ghee to a bubble, then add the sliced garlic. As it starts to turn golden, turn off the heat then return the vegetables to the pan and stir to coat well.

Arrange the vegetables on a large serving plate and lay the fish on top. Pour the dressing over the fish and serve with steamed jasmine rice.

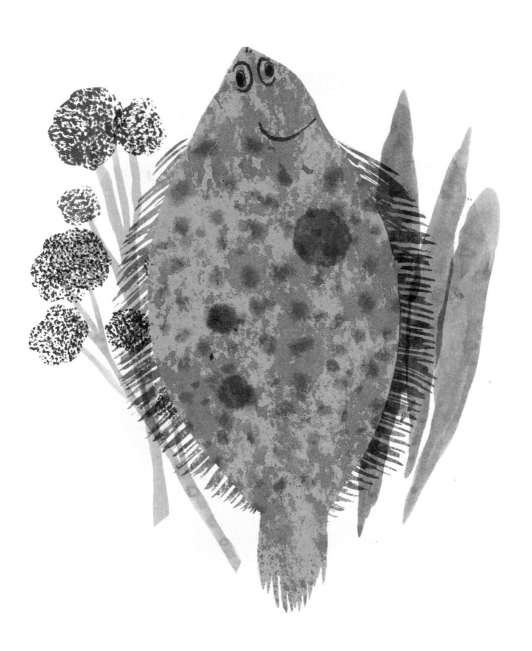

PANDAN AND COCONUT RICE PUDDING WITH CASSAVA

There is something especially comforting about rice pudding when the nights are still cold. Yet the grassy, nutty, vanilla flavour of pandan leaf promises a fresh and optimistic taste of spring. The texture of the cassava injects an element of surprise, like a sweet, waxy potato. Alternatively, you can also use lotus seeds, purple sweet potato, taro or pumpkin. This pudding can be made in advance, then reheated.

Serves 4

200g (7oz) glutinous rice, soaked for at least 30 minutes
400ml (14fl oz) coconut water
45g (1½oz) palm sugar
5 tbsp (2½oz) coconut cream, plus extra to serve

For the cassava:
150g (5½oz) cassava root, peeled
20g (¾oz) fresh pandan leaves, washed and cut into 10cm (4in) strips
100ml (3½fl oz)coconut water

First, prepare the cassava. Cut out any blackened sections, slice thinly, then steam for 20 minutes.

To make the pandan extract, blend the prepared leaves with the coconut water. Strain the juice through a sieve into a container and discard the debris.

To make the pudding, put the drained rice, coconut water and palm sugar in a saucepan over a medium heat. Cover the pan and bring to the boil, then reduce the heat to its lowest setting. Add the steamed cassava and coconut cream and cook, stirring occasionally, for 15 minutes. Add the pandan extract, folding it through the rice, and cook for a further 5 minutes.

Serve warm with a little extra coconut cream and some sliced fresh fruit if you fancy it.

Reading List

Kate Winslow and Guy Ambrosino,
Onions Etcetera
Recipes for every edible allium, from za'atar onion petals with beetroot and labneh to spring onion sesame pancakes.

Gill Meller,
Root, Stem, Leaf, Flower
A celebration of seasonal British produce, from spring shoots to autumn fruits, with stunning photography and lyrical interludes.

Fiona Beckett,
Fiona Beckett's Cheese Course
Nothing beats a plate of cheese and a glass of wine. Tips and ideas for the perfect cheeseboard, pairing drinks from port to cider, and how to throw a wine and cheese party.

Bert Blaize and Claire Strickett,
Which Wine When
An everyday guide to what to drink with the food you love, with expert wine matches for everything from takeaways and snacks to Sunday lunches, cheese and desserts.

Durkhanai Ayubi,
Parwana
A family's story of their homeland and a fascinating insight into Afghanistan's rich heritage, interwoven with the traditional recipes that give a vital sense of belonging to those displaced by war.

Frederik van Oudenhoven,
With Our Own Hands
A unique and intimate portrait of the Pamir Mountains of Afghanistan and Tajikistan, told through timeworn recipes and the agricultural history of one of the world's most isolated civilisations.

Uyen Luu,
Vietnamese
Simple Vietnamese food to cook at home. Try the sizzling crêpes with prawns followed by the pandan ice cream.

April

April can fool us into thinking
spring has truly arrived, only to dash
our hopes with endless showers.
The hungry gap may temper our
kitchen ambitions, but there is sharp
sorrel and the crisp, peppery bite of
watercress and radish to enliven our
palates – and wild confetti will soon
be thrown from blossoming fruit trees
to remind us of the bounty to come.

IN SEASON

Agretti
Dandelion flowers
Good King Henry
Gorse
Hop shoots
Morels
Outdoor rhubarb

Pea shoots
Radishes
Rock samphire
Sea spinach
Sorrel
Watercress

Watercress

Fresh, bright and wonderfully peppery, the petalled green leaves of watercress are testament to the rising sap; a hint of spring while the hungry gap lingers on. A member of the mustard family, watercress is more subtly spiced, its warming bitterness once thought to purify the blood. It was adored by the Victorians, who ate some 15 million bunches each year in London alone, often sold on the streets by young 'watercress girls' and eaten as a walking lunch.

Once harvested, watercress quickly wilts and loses its sweetness, leaving a less appealing, hot, bitter flavour. Choose vigorous bunches of young cress, bright green with small leaves and thin stems, avoiding any that are flowering – though Dorothy Hartley assures us 'the knowledgeable prefer their cress "sunburnt" – that is slightly older – when the leaves have acquired a delicate bronze'.

Watercress makes a fine soup, served hot or chilled, and a refreshing, brilliant green purée that can be swirled into sauces for scallops, salmon or roasted new potatoes. Jane Grigson serves her soup with cheese straws or fingers of grilled cheese on toast, a habit worth adopting, while Joyce Molyneux adds the scented sweetness of ripe pears, along with a little cream and lemon.

Grigson considers watercress sandwiches the best of all watercress dishes: 'Nothing can challenge the perfect combination of good bread, salty butter and peppery crisp watercress,' she asserts. Bacon, ham or chicken can be added, but there is a quiet understatement to using a single ingredient in its prime. Just be sure to cut thick slices of bread and use plenty of cress 'so that it bursts cheerfully out at the sides'.

Watercress adds pep to leftovers; a salad of cold roast chicken with a mustardy dressing is reason enough to cook a bigger bird. And there's no end to the salads that benefit from its punchy flavour: try it tossed with fennel, sliced oranges and a salty hit of feta; with beetroot and walnuts and a fruity vinegar; or with new season morels simmered in cream. Its peppery notes means it pairs well with beef – try watercress relish chopped with shallots and horseradish on your steak – and it adds spice to a pesto for crostini, pasta or crudités.

Viewed in a different light, watercress can be used as a herb, flavouring sauces and butters such as the French *sauce verte* and *beurre montpellier*. It's worth remembering when you want a mix of *fines herbes* for an omelette too. Versatile and full of flavour, watercress is so much more than just a frilly garnish.

WATERCRESS GIRLS

In its Victorian heyday, the cries of 'Wa-tercrease, wa-tercrease, fine fresh wa-tercrease!' chimed out among exhortations to buy muffins, dried fish, jacket potatoes and penny toys. Most of the sellers were 'watercress girls', often much younger than the legal minimum working age of 10 years old. School attendance was not compulsory and the poorest families, often living in one-room slums, needed their children to earn, hopeful that their youthful innocence would appeal to buyers.

Everyday life for the watercress girls was tough. Dressed in rags in the cold early-morning air, they often stood outside the city's markets for hours, waiting until the main traders had bought their stock. Running the cresses under street water-pumps to keep them looking fresh gave the girls chilblains, and there was little prospect of food until they had sold at least some of their watercress bunches.

They may have brought a taste of the countryside to the streets of London, but the thousands of young watercress sellers led lives that were anything but bucolic. For all their emphasis on society morality, it took the Victorians a long time to see the true, desperate picture. But their wretched lot would eventually inspire a major charitable movement, with the 'Watercress and Flower Girls' Christian Mission' marking the beginning of one of the most meaningful philanthropic organisations of the time.

MAKE AHEAD

Cherry blossom

Capture the cherry tree's fleeting flowers in sugar, spirits or vinegar to enjoy in summer when the fresh fruit arrives. Pick flowers that are just starting to open and simmer in water and sugar to make a syrup to flavour cakes and jams, or to drizzle on fresh cherries when they ripen in July.

The Vinegar Revival
by Angela Clutton

My kitchen is small. I mean *small* small. Small London flat small. There are cupboards that can barely contain the pots and pans and roasting dishes, crammed to the hilt and at risk of falling whenever a door is opened. And yet, there's a cupboard just by the hob, barely an arm-stretch away from whatever I am cooking, where my glory of vinegars from across the world luxuriate in (relative) space.

Right at the front is a good bottle of Andalusian sherry vinegar that can truly make a dish sing: its depth of flavour reflects the *solera* cask-ageing these vinegars share with the famous sherries of the region. Tucked behind it are wine vinegars from particular grapes and regions; fruit vinegars from orchard-rich lands; rice vinegars from grains you might only find in far-away farming communities – vinegars whose flavours owe as much to their *terroir* as to the quality of their base ingredients.

You can't rush a good vinegar: it has to mature. Turning alcohol into vinegar barely takes any time at all, given the right bacteria and equipment, but it results in a very mediocre product best relegated to pickling. The best require artistry, skill and patience at every step of the process to convert the sugars of the base ingredients to alcohol, allowing the aceto-bacteria fermentation magic to unfold naturally, and then slowly ageing the resulting vinegar in casks.

You can make your own vinegar at home from leftover wine and it's fun to do. But so is seeking out the global craftspeople who are honing centuries of vinegar-making skills. These are the vinegars to prize and to embrace in all your cooking.

VINEGARS TO LOOK OUT FOR

Malt vinegar

Modern producers are resurrecting Britain's Victorian-era boom in malt vinegar. Traditional production techniques and heritage grains make for superior malt vinegars that are just as good for your Friday night fish and chips as for whisking into mayonnaise and gravies.

Wine vinegars

Look beyond the generic red and white wine vinegars and seek out bottles produced from specific grapes or styles – perhaps merlot, muscat or a dessert wine, such as Sauternes. Special mention goes to champagne vinegar, perfect for dressing fish and seafood dishes, especially crab.

Fruit vinegars

The best fruits make for the best fruit vinegars: provenance matters. Sicilian melons make a light and zesty vinegar for marinating fish and drizzling over slices of fresh melon with cracked black pepper; while aromatic Austrian cherries make a vinegar that is perfect with game.

Vegetable vinegars

Vinegars made with vegetables are rare – so if you see one, buy it! My favourite is made with asparagus, pressed and fermented to make asparagus wine and then re-fermented into an intense and delicious vinegar. Use in salad dressings or partner with anything you know goes well with asparagus. It's also surprisingly good in a G&T.

Sherry vinegar

The final word goes to sherry vinegar because it really is my desert-island vinegar. It doesn't have to be fancy, but it does need to have the 'DO' label to signify barrel ageing. Use for meat marinades, sauces, dressings, and add to almost any stew or soup.

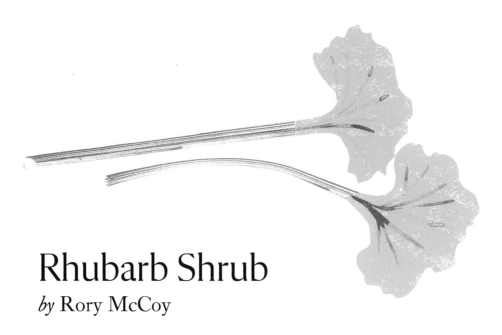

Rhubarb Shrub
by Rory McCoy

```
1kg (2lb 4oz) rhubarb, cut into 1cm (½in) pieces
500g (1lb 2oz) unrefined caster sugar
400ml (14fl oz) unpasteurised apple cider vinegar
400ml (14fl oz) filtered water
1 vanilla pod, split lengthways
```

Put the rhubarb, sugar, vinegar and water in a saucepan over a low heat. Use the tip of a knife to scrape the vanilla seeds into the pan and discard the pod. Stir immediately so that they separate and don't clump.

Bring to the boil slowly, then reduce the heat and simmer for 15 minutes. Allow to cool completely, then pour into a sterilised jar. Seal and place in the fridge.

Leave for 5–10 days to let the flavours come together, tasting every few days to see when it's ready – you're looking for a good balance between sweetness, tart fruit and acidity. When you're happy with the flavour, make a bag by tying the corners of a muslin square together and then hanging it over a large bowl. Carefully pour the liquid into the bag and leave to strain. You're looking for clear liquid, so this will take a good few hours or you can leave it overnight.

Once strained, take a small handful of the pulp and whisk it back into your liquid – this will add texture and colour. Store the shrub in a sterilised jar in the fridge for up to three months. Enjoy it as you would a cordial, usually diluted 1:2 parts with sparkling water, or simply to taste. Alternatively, add about 25ml (1fl oz) to sparkling wine to make a rhubarb Bellini.

The Bun also Rises

by Letitia Clark

The first bun I ever fell in love with was small, yolk-yellow and studded with raisins; smooth matte on top, ragged at the sides, where you could peel away strips of the softest, saffron-stained dough. I got it from the post office.

When I was little, we went to Lerryn in Cornwall every year. Lerryn was all moss, mud and mussels, snails and swans. We ate scampi crisps and saffron buns. The post office was at the bottom of a steep hill, on the way to the stepping stones across the river.

I bought a bag of buns, beaming bright through the plastic packet. The first I ate crossing the river, hopping over the honeycomb-shaped stones, throwing crumbs to the mean Muscovy ducks. It tasted like sun-baked hay, honey and hot dust – the raisins plump and damp, the dough soft and sweet – a flavour and colour so foreign in that cold, green-grey landscape where blue mussels clung to the rocks, smudged with estuary mud, and weeds swayed in the water like beards in the wind. The others we toasted at our little holiday cottage and ate with slabs of butter, salty and thick as a thumb.

Saffron buns are a Cornish oddity; no one really knows why they are made there. Perhaps in days of tin trading, the Cornish acquired the spice from the Phoenicians, as early as 400 BC, and baked it into their cakes, loaves and buns.

I could measure out my life in buns: those first holiday buns from the post office; the Hot Crosses for Good Friday, spiced and speckled with dried fruit and peel; Belgian buns from the local bakery, sticky with white fondant icing and crowned with a red glacé cherry, inescapably nipple-like; the iced bun fingers we bought from the supermarket by the half dozen.

As a young undergraduate I dreamed of opening a bookshop-cum-bakery called 'The Bun also Rises', where the smell of freshly baked buns would mingle with the must of books, and I would sit ensconced in a tattered armchair eating warm buns, dripping butter onto purple passages. Perhaps happily, this pipe dream has remained just that, but buns of all shapes and sizes will always occupy a soft, round place in my heart and home, plumply and proudly rising to every occasion.

EASTER BUNS OF EUROPE

Buns of all shapes and sizes appear across various cultures and cuisines, from Swedish *kanelbullar* to Roman *maritozzi* and the Sicilian bun-with-a-bun *brioche col tuppo*. The Easter connection is widespread, and most buns mushroom into existence around Lent. Here are some European offerings.

Italian colomba pasquale

The dove-shaped sister of panettone and *pandoro*, this giant Milanese bun is the traditional Easter treat in Italy. Its soft buttery dough is often flecked with candied peel, and it has a distinctive and addictively crunchy topping of almonds and sugar.

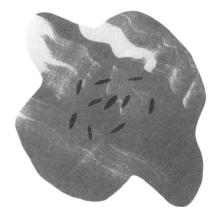

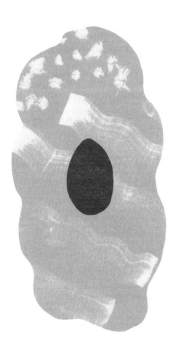

Greek tsoureki

A fragrant plaited Easter bread topped with flaked almonds. The three separate strands represent the Holy Trinity. Shiny, golden and with a soft eggy crumb, the enriched bread dough is flavoured distinctly with mahleb (an aromatic spice ground from the stones of the St Lucie cherry) and mastic (a tree resin).

Bulgarian kozunak

Similar to *tsoureki*, though often made without spices, *kozunak* is another plaited brioche popular at Easter in Bulgaria, Romania, Moldova and other parts of Eastern Europe. In Greece, where it is called *cozonac*, it is often filled with spices, honey and walnuts. The leavened dough, enriched with eggs, milk and sugar, is often flecked with rum-soaked raisins, and the resulting sweet bread is eaten in thick slices with coffee or tea.

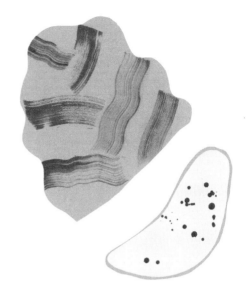

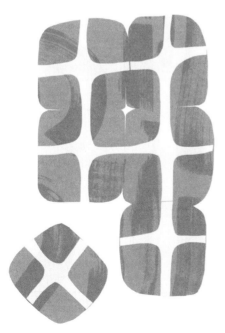

British hot cross buns

The British offering is delicately spiced with cinnamon, nutmeg and clove. The crowning cross and spiced dough were probably an Easter-themed adaptation of traditional London buns, which have been made by bakeries since the 1850s. Folklore claimed that buns baked on Good Friday would never go mouldy, and UK supermarkets now sell these spiced offerings all year round in a range of fancy flavours, from salted caramel to cranberry. Unsurprisingly, they do go off.

A Menu for April
by Marianna Leivaditaki

BRAISED ARTICHOKES WITH OLIVE, SUNDRIED TOMATO AND WALNUT SAUCE

Globe artichokes are one of my favourite vegetables. I grew up next to fields of them in Crete, eating them raw with sea salt and lemon, or in a lamb stew with broad beans. This dish is a combination of many things I love eating – olives, capers, sun-dried tomatoes – all punchy ingredients with bold flavours.

```
Serves 4

4 large globe artichokes
4 tbsp olive oil
1 garlic clove
200ml (7fl oz) white wine
Mint leaves, freshly chopped, to garnish

For the sauce:
6 Romano peppers
50g (1¾oz) green olives, stoned
70g (2½oz) sun-dried tomatoes
1 tbsp capers
60g (2¼oz) walnuts, lightly toasted
4 tbsp olive oil
1 tsp Turkish chilli flakes
1 tbsp pomegranate molasses
2 tsp red wine vinegar
1 slice of good-quality bread, fried gently in olive oil
```

Preheat the oven to 200°C/400°F/gas mark 6.

Prepare the artichokes by removing the tough outer leaves until you reach the paler inner ones. Cut off the top about two-thirds down, where there is a natural indentation, and discard. Use a teaspoon to scrape out the hairy chokes. Trim off the stalks, unless they are very tender, and remove any remaining outer leaves from the hearts.

Place a pan over a medium heat and add the olive oil and garlic. Put the artichokes in the pan, stem-side up, and fry gently until they turn golden. Pour in the wine and enough water to cover them halfway. Put a lid on the pan and cook for about 20 minutes until the artichokes are tender and the liquid has almost evaporated. Keep warm.

Meanwhile, roast the whole red peppers in the oven for 20 minutes. Remove and place in a bowl covered with a plate or lid. When cool enough to handle, peel and discard the stalk, skin and seeds.

Make the sauce by pulsing the peppers with the remaining ingredients in a food processor. It should be quite thick but not paste-like. If too thick, add some more oil and a splash of water.

Place the warm artichokes on a plate and pour over the sauce. Sprinkle with the freshly chopped mint and serve with some fresh bread on the side.

SLOW-COOKED LAMB AND MIZITHRA FILO PIE

I have grown up hand in hand with this dish. Not something cooked in our home, where fish was always the protagonist, but a dish we often went in search of in the tiny villages at the foot of the Cretan mountains. The filo pastry and mizithra cheese were always freshly made by hand, and the animals enjoyed a good life in the fields below. Traditionally, the bones are left on the meat and included in the pie, so the act of eating it becomes a hands-on affair, but here I remove them first. This is a dish that celebrates spring, when the young lamb meat is buttery and sweet.

Serves 4–6

1kg (2lb 4oz) lamb shanks on the bone
1 carrot, trimmed and roughly chopped
1 leek, trimmed and roughly chopped
1 celery stick, roughly chopped
2 tbsp olive oil
1 onion, chopped
100ml (3½fl oz) white wine
400g (14oz) mizithra cheese, or fresh goat's curd or ricotta
1 large bunch of fresh mint, leaves picked and finely chopped
1 egg, beaten
2 tbsp white sesame seeds
Sea salt and freshly ground black pepper

```
For the filo:
400g (14oz) plain flour, plus extra for rolling
100ml (3½fl oz) olive oil, plus extra for greasing
1 tsp fine sea salt
A shot of raki or grappa, or a splash of vinegar
About 100ml (3½fl oz) tepid water
```

Place the lamb shanks in a saucepan and cover with water. Add 2 teaspoons of salt, along with the carrot, leek and celery. Cook over a medium heat for about 1 hour, or until the meat is tender and falling off the bone. Set aside.

Meanwhile, make the filo pastry. Put the flour in a bowl and add the olive oil, salt and raki. Make a well in the centre and start adding the water, little by little. Bring it all together, kneading with your hands until you have a lovely soft, silky, elastic dough. This dough does not need a lot of kneading, so stop as soon as the right texture is achieved. Place a damp cloth over the dough and let it sit for 30 minutes or more.

Heat a small pan over a medium heat and add the olive oil and the onion. Season with salt and pepper and cook gently until sweet and translucent. Add the wine and cook for a further 2 minutes, then remove from the heat. Transfer the onion to a large bowl, then add the mizithra cheese and the chopped mint. Pull the lamb meat off the bone into smallish pieces using your hands. Add the meat to the bowl with the cheese, mint and onion. Set aside while you roll the pastry.

Preheat the oven to 180°C/350°F/gas mark 4 and grease a large baking tray. Divide the dough in half, keeping one half under the damp cloth. Dust the work surface with flour and roll out one piece as thinly as you can without it breaking.

Carefully transfer your rolled-out sheet onto the baking tray. It should overlap the tray on all sides. Roll out the remaining dough, again as thinly as possible. Put the filling mixture on the first sheet and cover it to form a pie using the second sheet of pastry. Cut the excess dough around the tray using a sharp knife and tuck in the rest to seal in the filling. Brush the top with egg wash and sprinkle with sesame seeds. Cut a cross in the centre of your pie to allow steam to escape. Cook for about 45 minutes, or until the filo is golden brown and all the juices have evaporated.

Allow the pie to cool a little before serving. Cut into portion sizes and serve with a leafy salad dressed with lots of lemon juice, olive oil and salt.

GREEK-STYLE TRIFLE WITH CARDAMOM CUSTARD, RHUBARB AND PISTACHIOS

This pudding is definitely not your traditional trifle: no jelly, no super-sweet 'granny's' sherry, and the cream is whipped with yogurt and sprinkled with pistachios. The addition of sweet Greek wine and brandy is what makes it for me.

Serves 4–6

For the sponge:
125g (4½oz) unsalted butter, softened
125g (4½oz) caster sugar
3 eggs, separated
200g (7oz) Greek yogurt
Zest of 1 unwaxed orange
225g (8oz) self-raising flour
2 tsp baking powder

For the custard:
400ml (14fl oz) double cream
200ml (7fl oz) whole milk
Seeds from 1 vanilla pod
2 cardamom pods, crushed
6 egg yolks
100g (3½oz) caster sugar
1 tsp fine semolina

For the rhubarb:
700g (1lb 9oz) rhubarb (about 6–8 stems), cut into 4cm (1¼in) pieces
200g caster sugar
200ml (7fl oz) fresh orange juice

To assemble the trifle:
150ml (5fl oz) double cream
2 tbsp caster sugar
150g (5fl oz) yogurt
50ml (2fl oz) sweet wine (I use Greek samos)
50ml (2fl oz) Greek brandy (Metaxa)
100g (3½oz) shelled pistachios, crushed

First make the cake. Preheat the oven to 180°C/350°F/gas mark 4 and grease and line a Swiss roll tin or similar-sized rectangular cake tin.

Beat the butter and sugar together in a stand mixer until pale and creamy. Add the egg yolks, one at a time. Then add the yogurt and orange zest. Turn your mixer to the lowest setting and slowly add the flour and baking powder. Transfer the contents to a separate large bowl.

Wash and dry your mixer bowl and beaters really well. Whisk the egg whites until soft peaks form. Gently fold the egg whites into the cake mixture and scrape into your greased cake tin, levelling the surface. Bake for about 30 minutes or until a skewer inserted into the middle comes out clean.

Remove from the oven, but do not switch it off. Allow to stand for 5 minutes, then turn out onto a cooling rack. When completely cold, cut into 1cm (½in) slices.

To make the custard, put the cream, milk, vanilla seeds and cardamom in a pan over a gentle heat and bring to a soft boil. Reduce the heat and let the cream simmer. Using an electric mixer, whisk the egg yolks with the sugar and semolina until pale and creamy. Remove the cream from the heat and, working very quickly, whisk in the egg mix. Return to the heat, whisking continuously over the lowest setting for another couple of minutes or until the custard thickens. Transfer to a dish and chill in the fridge.

Put the rhubarb in a large ovenproof dish. Pour the orange juice into the dish and sprinkle the sugar over the top. Bake for 10–15 minutes or until just soft.

To assemble the trifle, whip the cream with the sugar until soft peaks form. Add the yogurt and continue to whip until everything comes together.

Place a layer of the sponge slices in the base of a serving bowl (I have a 20cm (8in) square ceramic square dish I like to use for this). Pour over as little or as much alcohol as you like.

Follow with a thick layer of custard and then repeat with another layer of sponge and custard.

Finish with a satisfactory layer of the whipped cream and yogurt, followed by the rhubarb and some of its syrup, then sprinkle generously with pistachios. Keep in the fridge until ready to serve.

Reading List

Joyce Molyneux,
The Carved Angel Cookery Book
Good, honest cooking from one of the forerunners of the modern British food movement and a passionate advocate for local, seasonal ingredients. Watercress recipes include a mousseline with eggs, a soup with pears and a sauce with scallops in filo pastry.

Henry Mayhew,
London Labour and the London Poor
A vivid account of London's working classes in the mid-nineteenth century with interviews and anecdotal reports on almost every aspect of working life, including the 'watercress girls'.

Lillie O'Brien,
Five Seasons of Jam
Adventurous ideas for preserving the seasons. Flick to the spring chapter to learn how to make cherry blossom syrup and *sakurayu* tea.

Angela Clutton,
The Vinegar Cupboard
A celebration of the cultural histories and culinary potential of vinegar from balsamic to coconut, encouraging readers to acquire as many varieties as they can fit in their kitchen cupboards.

Clare Lattin and Tom Hill,
Ducksoup Cookbook
The wisdom of simple cooking from a tiny neighbourhood restaurant in Soho. Pickles and ferments feature prominently, with recipes for krauts, kombuchas and drinking vinegars.

Letitia Clark,
La Vita è Dolce
Italian-inspired desserts from the author's time living in Sardinia, and an appreciation of the sweet things in life. Try the cream-filled *maritozzi* buns for an indulgent breakfast.

Elizabeth David,
English Bread and Yeast Cookery
An unrivalled history of breadmaking in England, first published in 1977, with an exhaustive collection of recipes for everything from plain brown wholemeal to saffron cakes, drop scones and croissants. The hot cross bun recipe is a classic.

Marianna Leivaditaki,
Aegean
Cretan recipes from the mountains to the sea, and a delicious evocation of the chef's childhood home.

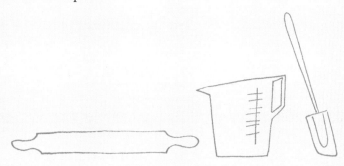

May

A gentle interlude between the seasons, May brings some of the most exciting British produce to the table. Celebrate with spears of asparagus dipped into soft-boiled eggs, tiny new potatoes tossed in butter, and the joy of plain cakes with an afternoon cup of tea. Salads are also at their tenderest – blousy and soft or crisp – bringing freshness and vitality to the simplest of dishes.

IN SEASON

Asparagus
Daylilies
Dulse
Elderflower
Green garlic
Hispi cabbage
Honeyberries

Jersey Royals
Padrón peppers
Rocket
Soft herbs
Sweet cicely
Wild onion

Jersey Royals

Tiny new potatoes break ground in May, a glimpse of heartier crops to come. Jersey Royals appear first with their nutty sweetness, waxy texture and fragile papery skins. Hailing from the island of Jersey, they share the same protected status as Cornish clotted cream, West Country Cheddar and champagne.

Potatoes are so rooted in our culinary heritage, it's strange to think how long they took to grace our tables. Medieval Britain had no potatoes, and even when they hit their stride in the eighteenth century, many still eyed them with suspicion. When potatoes were finally assimilated, they were often used for puddings. Danish *brunkartofler* still nod to this tradition, small boiled potatoes cooked with butter and sugar until they're coated in a golden caramel.

We love potatoes for their versatility, and Jerseys are no exception. Their firm texture makes them ideal for potato salads, dressed with a herbed vinaigrette or something creamy like homemade mayonnaise or crème fraîche. The secret is to dress when warm so they absorb all the flavour of the dressing. Scatter liberally with herbs – chervil, chives and dill all work well – or toss with sorrel for a fresh lemony zing. Something sharp accentuates their satisfying starchiness: try pickled walnuts, cornichons, shallots or spring onions.

It's tempting to go down the salty route too, adding crispy bacon, melting anchovies into butter, or smothering a plate of steaming orbs in glorious melted cheese. Simon Hopkinson even suggests serving new potatoes with caviar and chives – a luxurious snack to eat with champagne. But for the first Jersey Royals of the season, practise restraint and prepare a bowl with just butter and freshly chopped parsley, accompanied by a glass of wine.

MAKE AHEAD

Green garlic hot sauce

Early, immature garlic is tender and mild, even when raw, offering up a more mellow heat. Blitz both the stalks and bulbs with preserved lemons, green chillies, vinegar and salt, then leave at room temperature for a few days to kick-start fermentation. This vibrant spicy sauce will last at least a year in the fridge, ready to be splodged onto eggs, sandwiches, grilled meats and vegetables.

Potato Salad

by Emily Nunn

My favourite potato salad is whatever potato salad has landed in front of me at any given time. If I order a sandwich in a restaurant and it automatically comes with some on the side, I'm going to devour it – no questions asked. And when a kind person brings potato salad to a funeral reception I'm attending, I'll eat as much as I can swallow through my tears and grief.

I once believed that the only potato salad on the planet was the luscious mayonnaise-soaked, pickle-celery-onion-studded marvel I ate growing up in the American South – a lesser version of which you'll find in diners all over America. But when I grew up, the scales fell from my eyes.

At an art-student potluck in college, an enormous foil-draped bowl appeared on the picnic table, containing stuffed green olives, tinned smoked oysters and crushed almonds – clearly someone had raided their parents' cocktail party pantry back home – with slices of steamed new potatoes and spring onions, all dressed in soured cream. It seemed like pure insanity to me. I ate two servings and was sorry when I returned for a third to find the bowl empty.

But do I have plans to recreate that potato salad? No. Mainly because life is short and one must keep moving, ever onwards, in order to experience all the potato salad the world has given us – which is a lot. The potato, domesticated in Peru about 8,000 years ago, is one of a handful of vegetables eaten in practically every culture around the globe, and we dispatch more than 245 kilotons of them a year.

And this means – hallelujah! – potato salad shows up everywhere too. In Japan, it's a mashed affair with ham, cucumber, and Kewpie mayo (one of my favourites). *Huzarensalade*, from the Netherlands, is full of pickles, ham, apples and peas. The Polish version, *sałatka ziemniaczana*, includes fresh or pickled vegetables, boiled eggs and smoked meat, bound with soured cream and seasoned with dill. In China, potatoes are shredded, blanched, tossed with herbs and spring onions, and doused with hot chilli oil.

Food historians often point to the German (warm) and French (cold) versions we still eat today as the potato salad originals. But they also imply that these creations were meant to 'get rid of' leftover potatoes. *Get rid!* My god. I choose instead to believe we turn potatoes into salad because we have such tender feelings about the garden's gentlest, most accommodating vegetable, which has fed and comforted us for centuries. In a pageant of far flashier vegetables, potato salad is the spotlight-grabbing vehicle that allows the potato to sing its soothing song.

How to Dress
by Jess Elliott Dennison

There's a noticeable shift in my kitchen as we approach the promising days of May. As I pack away my jumpers and woolly layers, I find I leave cooking behind too. Instead, I simply assemble ingredients for lunch and dinner – for now is the time for salads.

There's a purity and gentleness about May's ingredients. The verdant greens of asparagus, peas, spring onions and watercress look so pleasing alongside blushing pink radishes and something pale and creamy: a crushed Jersey Royal, a chalky-white soft cheese, a herby yogurt dressing.

This isn't the time for endless stirring, overcomplicating or trying to impress. Instead, I urge you to keep things as simple as possible by gently jumbling a few of the season's best ingredients onto a platter, then stepping out into the garden, or at least over to a sunny spot with the window open.

BEST DRESSINGS

Herby Yogurt

Perfect pairing: peas or broad beans, sprouting broccoli and butter beans.

Blitz together 125g (4 ½oz) natural yogurt, ¼ small garlic clove, a small bunch of basil, dill and mint (leaves only), 1½ tablespoons olive oil, a pinch of sea salt and the zest and juice of ½ lemon. Toss through some gently steamed broccoli, a handful of fresh peas or broad beans and a drained can or small jar of butter beans, and tumble onto a platter with a few capers and some toasted pine nuts. Any extra dressing can be mopped up with crusty bread.

Wild Garlic Aioli

Perfect pairing: Jersey Royals or new potatoes, cornichons and watercress.

Whisk together 1 egg yolk, 1½ teaspoon Dijon mustard, ½ minced garlic clove, pinch of salt, and zest and juice of ½ lemon. Drop by drop, pour in 300ml (10fl oz) cold-pressed rapeseed or light olive oil, continuously whisking until very thick. Stir in a handful of finely chopped wild garlic. Boil a small pan of Jersey Royals or new potatoes until tender, then drain and toss the wild garlic aioli through the still-warm potatoes and tip onto a platter. Scatter over some roughly chopped cornichons and a handful of crisp, fresh watercress. Top with some peeled soft-boiled, jammy-centred eggs if you fancy, too.

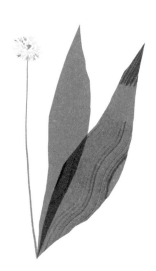

Crispy Rosemary and Shallot

Perfect pairing: farfalle pasta, asparagus, lettuce and Parma ham.

Fry 6 slices of Parma ham in a hot pan until really crispy. Remove the crispy ham, then fry 3 roughly chopped rosemary sprigs in the rendered ham fat. Remove from the heat then stir in ½ tablespoon olive oil, 3 tablespoons vinegar, a pinch of sugar and sea salt, and a finely diced shallot. Toss a few handfuls of cooked, drained and chilled farfalle onto a platter along with a few handfuls of fresh peas and a shredded Cos lettuce or some wild rocket. Use a peeler to shave over some raw asparagus, then spoon over the dressing and top with the crispy ham.

Lemon and Mint Ricotta

Perfect pairing: radish, shaved fennel and Marcona almonds.

Blitz 250g (9oz) ricotta with a handful of mint leaves, the zest of a lemon and a squeeze of its juice, along with a pinch of salt, until smooth and beautifully flecked with the mint. Spoon onto the base of a platter, then use a mandolin to shave over a handful of radishes and a small fennel bulb (or very finely slice with a knife). Crush then scatter some deliciously salty Marcona almonds on top.

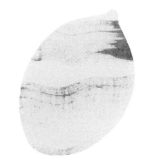

The Joy of Plain Cakes
by Rachel Roddy

Before its drastic renovation, the bar opposite our building in Rome had two bright red doors, each with a porthole window, the effect of which was to make the doors seem like eyes. It was hard to leave our main gate and not feel watched. And invited! Which, for someone who often needs coffee, was usually welcome. The rubber-bottomed doors swished as they swung inwards, revealing a small cash desk and a zinc-topped counter about three metres long. On one end of it sat a small glass cabinet, filled with pastries in the morning and ham sandwiches in the afternoon, and a large plastic dome protecting a ring cake.

Standing at the bar in a bar is the best sort of waiting. I first had this thought when I was about seven, while waiting for a shandy and bag of crisps in my granny's pub in Manchester, enjoying the noise, movement and anticipation. It's a thought I have carried through my life. At the zinc counter, I would stand watching the two baristas work, pressing coffee grounds into nests and twisting them into place, steaming milk, slicing lemons, levering the caps from triangular bottles of Campari soda, then emptying the red fizz into glasses.

The espresso and cappuccino produced were often slightly too strong for me, and they never had any ice. But that didn't matter, because I was standing at a familiar bar and there was ring cake, or what my other grandma might have referred to as a plain, or cut-and-come-again cake, although she never made rings, rather rounds or loaves, and often added seeds. The ring on the bar was three times the

size of one you might make at home, deep gold on the outside, butter-yellow within. Although it didn't know butter, rather vegetable oil. Also flour, eggs, milk, sugar, baking powder and orange essence. I know because the ingredients were written on the sticker stuck to the side of the dome.

An inch-thick slice would arrive on a small orange plate, rocking gently before settling on the zinc counter. I would break a corner off, then squeeze it before eating, wondering if there was an extra preservative, because even when the cake had been there a few days, it retained the resistant bounce, broke rather than crumbled, had fat crumbs rather than dry.

My grandma loved to chase the last crumbs of plain cake round the plate with her finger, before pressing gently to catch them. She was devoted to tea, but also loved Madeira or sweet sherry; after all, the drink is as important as the cake. Plain cake and sherry, she thought, was the best sort of eating, and I agree, especially after the best sort of waiting.

Sadly, I don't stand at that zinc counter anymore. Apparently another customer saved it from the dump when they renovated. I wonder what happened to the red doors like eyes, the cash desk designed like a fairground booth, the dome that protected a plain cake.

Madeira Cake

by Mary Berry

This is a rich, densely textured sponge cake. It is essential that the butter is a creamy, spreading consistency before mixing the ingredients together. If the cake has a slight dip in the centre when it comes out of the oven, simply turn it out onto baking paper on a cooling rack and leave it upside down. The action of gravity and the weight of the cake will level the top while it cools.

```
175g (6oz) unsalted butter, softened
175g (6oz) caster sugar
225g (8oz) self-raising flour
50g (1¾oz) ground almonds
3 large eggs
Finely grated zest of 1 lemon
A thin slice of citron peel
```

Preheat the oven to 180°C/350°F/gas mark 4. Grease a deep 18-cm (7-in) round cake tin and line the base with baking paper.

Put the butter, sugar, flour, ground almonds, eggs and grated lemon zest into a large bowl. Beat for 1 minute to mix thoroughly. Pour into the prepared tin and level the surface.

Bake for 30 minutes, then place the slice of citron peel on top of the cake and continue cooking for a further 30–45 minutes, or until a skewer inserted into the centre comes out clean. Leave to cool in the tin for 10 minutes, then turn out, peel off the baking paper and finish cooling on a wire rack.

A SPIRITED INVENTION

The true cake of Madeira is the *bolo de mel*, a rich spiced honey cake considered the island's oldest dessert. Made with yeasted dough, it can take days to make and keeps remarkably well, the sugar-cane 'honey' (treacle), nuts and dried fruit helping it to last the year. British Madeira cake, however, is named after the wine it was served with rather than the recipe's origin. A simple plain sponge, rich with butter, it became popular in nineteenth-century England, enjoyed mid-morning with a small glass of Madeira wine. Recipes for the cake started to be recorded around 1840, with a version published in Eliza Acton's *Modern Cookery For Private Families* in 1845. The most understated of cakes, its popularity has continued at teatime, its dense butteriness inviting you to cut 'just one more slice' until it has miraculously disappeared.

A Menu for May
by Anna Tobias

ASPARAGUS AND HOLLANDAISE

I realise this may not sound like the most innovative recipe, and in truth it is not.
However, I honestly think that the arrival of asparagus is one of the most exciting
moments of the year, and as such, I believe that the simpler the preparation,
the better. An asparagus spear dipped into a luxurious, velvety hollandaise is a
moment of total perfection.

Serves 4

24 green asparagus spears
4 egg yolks
300g (10½oz) unsalted butter, melted
A good squeeze of lemon juice
Sea salt and ground white pepper

Holding the asparagus towards its base, gently bend each spear so that the woody
end snaps off. Wash well.

To make the hollandaise, place the egg yolks in a heatproof bowl over a pan of
barely simmering water. Add a small splash of water (about a teaspoonful) and
whisk together until the yolks are thick and frothy. Very slowly whisk in the
melted butter in a thin stream until the sauce has the consistency of yogurt. Add
a squeeze of lemon and season with salt and white pepper. Take off the heat and
keep warm.

Boil the asparagus in salted water for about 4 minutes. You want them to be tender
– neither crunchy nor mushy. A good way to test this is to give the middle of the
asparagus spear a squeeze with your fingers; it should just yield to the pressure.

Drain the asparagus well, then arrange on a serving dish and pour over lashings
of hollandaise. Some bread for mopping up is a wise idea.

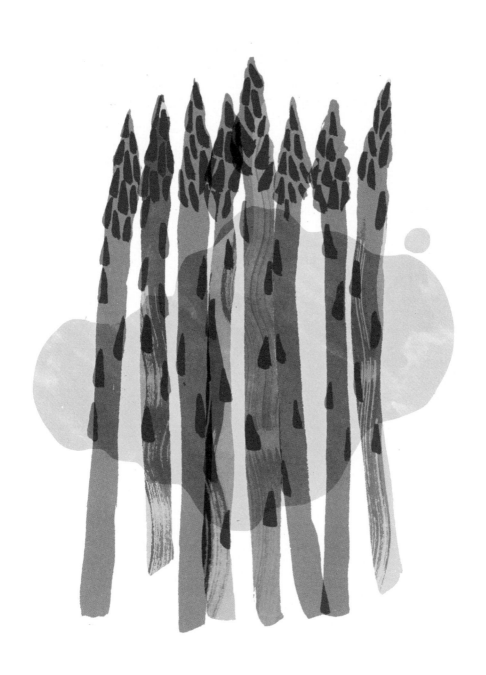

SLOW-ROAST DUCK LEGS WITH BACON AND ONIONS

There is something incredibly moreish about the combination of rich duck, salty bacon and the sweetness of marsala. It's become a bit of a dinner party staple for me, especially because you can take your eye off it (purposefully or by accident) and the results will still be great – the duck legs are happy to tick over.

Serves 4

4 duck legs
150g (5½oz) lardons
80g (2¾oz) button onions, peeled and left whole
½ bunch of sage, leaves picked
225ml (8fl oz) dry marsala
100ml (3½fl oz) water
2 bay leaves
Sea salt and freshly ground black pepper

Preheat the oven to 170°C/340°F/gas mark 3½.

Choose a cast-iron casserole or a baking dish that will accommodate the duck legs in a single layer. Season the duck legs with salt and pepper and place in the casserole (or use a frying pan) skin-side down. Place over a medium heat without any oil – the duck will release enough of its own fat to fry itself. Brown the legs well on both sides, then remove from the pan and set aside on a plate.

Add the lardons to the pan and fry until golden and crispy, then add the button onions and fry until golden. If there is too much fat in the pan, pour some (but not all) of it off. Sprinkle in the sage leaves and let them soak up the remaining fat and fry for a minute or two. Add the marsala and water to the pan and boil for 2 minutes.

Return the duck legs back to the casserole, skin-side up, along with the bay leaves (or, if using a baking dish, transfer all the ingredients to it now). Cover with baking paper and either the lid or a sheet of tightly wrapped foil and put in the oven.

Check the legs after 1½ hours. The meat should be cooked through and yielding. Insert a skewer through the thigh and gently twist – the flesh should ease away from the bone. If it is still a little tough, then return to the oven for another 30 minutes, checking again after 15.

Increase the oven temperature to 180°C/350°F/gas mark 4. Remove the lid and baking paper and cook for a furhter 10–15 minutes until the duck skin is crisp and golden.

Serve the duck with braised peas and Jersey Royals.

BRAISED PEAS AND LETTUCE

Serves 4

4 heads Little Gem lettuce
40g (1½oz) unsalted butter
1 bunch of spring onions, trimmed and roughly chopped
500g (1lb 2oz) fresh peas, shelled weight
Splash of sherry vinegar
1 small bunch of curly parsley, leaves picked and finely chopped
Sea salt and freshly ground black pepper

Discard the outer leaves of the lettuce if they look ragged. Cut the lettuce in half lengthways and swill around in water to wash the leaves and encourage any grit to fall out.

In a lidded pan that is big enough to hold the lettuce in one layer, melt 25g (1oz) of the butter and sweat the spring onions over a gentle heat for 5 minutes to soften them. Remove with a slotted spoon and set aside.

Place the lettuce halves, cut-side down, in the fat and very lightly brown. Turn cut-side up and scatter over the spring onions and peas. Give the pan a little shake so everything nestles in together. Season with salt and pepper.

Pour in 3 tablespoons of water. Cover with the lid and increase the heat to high for 2 minutes to get things going. Then reduce the heat right down and allow the peas and lettuce to slowly braise. Check the pan every so often to make sure it has not boiled dry – add extra water if needed.

After about 20 minutes, the peas should be cooked and sweet. Stir in the remaining butter and a small splash of sherry vinegar. Bubble for a minute, then remove from the heat. Check the seasoning and sprinkle with the parsley.

LEMON CRÈME FRAÎCHE ICE CREAM

This recipe is a total doddle. Low effort for high impact, which is always a pleasing result. If you don't have an ice-cream maker, don't worry. This ice cream doesn't need to be churned – it also comes out very scoopable if you just freeze it directly in a suitable container.

Serves 4

250g (9oz) caster sugar
Zest of 3 lemons and 175ml (6fl oz) juice (3–4 lemons)
175ml (6fl oz) double cream
400ml (14fl oz) crème fraîche

Put the sugar, lemon zest, cream and crème fraîche in a pan. Gently bring to the boil, then simmer for 3 minutes.

Stir in the lemon juice and churn according to your ice-cream maker's instructions, or simply pour into a container and freeze overnight.

Reading List

John Reader,
The Untold History of the Potato
The story of our favourite carb told through the tapestry of human history, from its origins and early cultivation to its mysterious arrival in Europe.

Emily Nunn,
The Comfort Food Diaries
A moving memoir, peppered with recipes, about finding comfort in the face of loss through travel, home-cooked food and the company of friends and family.

Jess Elliott Dennison,
Salad Feasts
Relaxed recipes for transforming ordinary salads into hearty feasts. Salads will never be dull again.

Rachel Roddy,
Five Quarters
Recipes and notes from the author's kitchen in Rome. Make the ricotta and lemon ring cake on a Sunday afternoon so Monday's breakfast is softened by cake.

Mary Berry,
Baking Bible
A definitive collection from the undisputed queen of cakes.

Noel Cossart,
Madeira, The Island Vineyard
A fascinating journey through 300 years of the Madeira wine trade and its island home, drawing on the author's personal experiences and family archives.

Susan Campbell,
English Cookery New and Old
A charming collection of menus inspired by the regional foods of England, such as 'An early spring picnic in the South West' and 'High tea in Yorkshire'.

June

Summer has finally arrived, and with it the first glorious fruits – gooseberries, strawberries, apricots – and the fervent search for ripe Indian mangoes. June is a happy month for the cook: fresh peas and broad beans flicked from their pods, simple salads and tarts spiked with the heady scent of soft herbs. Linger over meals and savour the warmth of the afternoon sun – food always tastes better when there are blue skies above.

IN SEASON

Apricots
Beetroot
Broad beans
Carrots
Garlic scapes
Gooseberries

Lettuce
New potatoes
Peas
Purslane
Strawberries

Peas

Peas represent everything that is special about the English summer – a sweet simple joy in a fleeting season. The best are bright green, tiny yet plump, so tender they don't really need cooking at all. It's important to eat them as fresh as possible, to beat the racing conversion from sugar to starch – pods that have lingered too long on the greengrocer's shelves will be dry, mealy and bitter. Peas are an unforgiving vegetable if not rushed from field to fork.

We love peas for their easy charm; undemanding of the cook and uncomplicated in their preparation. Cook them gently in butter, bacon fat or olive oil, or tumble them into a brief ferocious boil and serve with butter. Their sweetness works well with lamb, fish, ham and young cheeses, though it's difficult to find a plate they would not grace, sitting quietly beside the humblest ingredients or adding pops of green to pies, casseroles, risotto and pasta. Traditionally served with duck and green beans for Whit Sunday, peas have long been an early summer treat, often blitzed into emerald soups; braised with summer lettuces; lavished in cream. Etiquette dictates they should be pierced with the tines of a fork rather than scooping them up, even if they misbehave and bounce happily across the plate.

Fresh may now be considered best, but we predominantly ate dried peas until the sixteenth century, when Italian gardeners developed tender varieties and made sweet fresh peas fashionable. Dried peas and other pulses provided vital nutrition through long, hard winters in the form of pease pottage (a thick soup) and pease pudding (a savoury pudding boiled in cloth). In the 1920s, Clarence Birdseye discovered a method for quickly and efficiently freezing fresh peas, forever saving our meals from a lack of greenery. Frozen peas are so good, we now take the fresh ones for granted. But it's worth podding at least a handful or two to embrace the sweet joy of the season.

MUSHY PEAS

This chip shop favourite is now made with giant marrowfat peas, but before the nineteenth century, similar dishes such as pease pottage would have been made from dried field peas. A staple food throughout the Middle Ages, dried peas were often bought and boiled by street traders, sold hot with salt, pepper and vinegar as mushy peas are today.

WHAT TO DO WITH FRESH PEAS

- Eat straight from the pod with a sharp sheep's cheese such as Berkswell, pecorino or manchego.
- Stir-fry the tender shoots with garlic or use their curling tendrils to add delicious decoration to summer salads.
- Boil briefly in their pods and eat like edamame.
- Pair with broad beans and artichoke hearts for a traditional Roman *vignarola*.
- Crush with goat's cheese and mint and serve on toast with a sprinkling of sumac.
- Blitz with ginger, green chillies and spices and roll into Gujarati-style *kachori*.
- Make the classic Venetian risotto *risi e bisi*.
- Bring out their natural sweetness in desserts – try ice cream, mousse or a vanilla and pea cake with lemon icing.

MAKE AHEAD

Gooseberry sauce

Fresh gooseberries can be cooked very simply with butter and sugar to create a quick accompaniment for pork and oily fish, but for something more interesting, and more akin to an old-school brown sauce, try Mark Diacono's method of simmering gooseberries with white wine vinegar and light brown sugar, along with cloves, allspice, cinnamon and ground ginger. The resulting sauce, blitzed and bottled, has a hint of traditional farmhouse pickle about it. It keeps for at least six months in a cool, dark cupboard, ready to eat with sausages later in the year.

A Moveable Feast

by Mark Diacono

Walking empties my head. Putting one foot in front of the other convinces my brain it's doing enough to abandon its usual search for something to think about or do. It means *I am* in a way I'm otherwise not. Into this clarity ideas fall, creative leaps are made, perspective forms. *Solvitur ambulando*: it is solved by walking.

I don't stop for 'lunch' when I'm out for a long walk; I take frequent short breaks to sit in the grass, thickened with spring rain and the early warmth of summer, eating with a view of the trail I took while I was getting hungry. I'm rarely as content as in these moments.

Eating with the sky rather than a ceiling above makes everything taste better. When your mind is clear, the senses are alive to the change of season, and when you are truly hungry, it is an experience apart. When I bite into an apple with the same 'fot' of popping a new tin of tennis balls, my mouth waters in a way it usually reserves for a bacon roll. It tastes so completely of itself, I suspect because I am doing nothing more, thinking of nothing more, wanting nothing more than that apple, in the now, here.

WHAT TO TAKE ON A WALK

A walker's lunch requires consideration. It should comprise items that are either approaching spherical or can be pecked from the palm of one hand by the fingers and thumb of the other. A fork has no business in a rucksack; I take only a penknife. It feels important to cut something with a blade – a pie, a piece of fruit – ideally to be eaten straight from the knife. I am disinterested in any drink other than water, unless an excellent pub should present itself.

Rolls

Ham and mustard rolls to fill the stomach and clear the sinuses. They must be numerous (three minimum), made with soft bread, and with mustard of pipe-cleaning potency.

Scotch egg/sausage roll/pork pie

An item of what comedian Bob Mortimer calls 'pocket meat'. Every time I eat a Scotch egg I marvel at its brilliance: it is the perfect meal.

Crisps

They might be fancy or cheap; a lively salt and vinegar, most frequently.

A sweet treat

Flapjack or similar. Brownie is acceptable; crumbly cake most unwelcome. This is eaten first.

Virtuous snacks

Nuts, a banana, an apple: goodness for the home straight. Always eaten last. The banana invariably returns to my kitchen, uneaten and darker than when it left.

Foraging

I'm alive to the possibility of a few unexpected seasonal pleasures along the way. Later in the year, there might be hazelnuts and blackberries, but as spring gives way to summer, the leaves of Jack-by-the-hedge (hedge garlic) are at their succulent, plentiful best: the ham rolls are likely to benefit.

On Herbs

by Olia Hercules

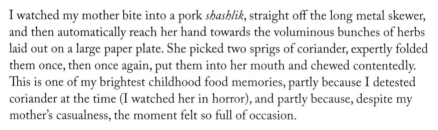

I watched my mother bite into a pork *shashlik*, straight off the long metal skewer, and then automatically reach her hand towards the voluminous bunches of herbs laid out on a large paper plate. She picked two sprigs of coriander, expertly folded them once, then once again, put them into her mouth and chewed contentedly. This is one of my brightest childhood food memories, partly because I detested coriander at the time (I watched her in horror), and partly because, despite my mother's casualness, the moment felt so full of occasion.

It was the late 1980s and we were in the south of Ukraine, near the pine woods by the River Dnipro. It was a typical Soviet picnic: meat marinated the night before and brought in a big lidded pot in the back of a Lada; dads and uncles fishing, mums and aunts slicing juicy tomatoes and cucumbers with penknives. Serving herbs whole in such big bunches wasn't necessarily part of Ukrainian eating culture – we are normally 'sprinklers of dill on everything' – but a lot of people we knew ate herbs like vegetables, especially if they cooked barbecue food, borrowing from Georgian or Azeri cuisine.

We did it because my dad's uncle married an Armenian woman. My dad even lived with them in Baku, Azerbaijan's capital, when he was twelve, during his parents' acrimonious divorce. Two of the things he always recounted from his unusual year in the Caucasus were Azeri and Armenian women baking flatbreads in *tandyr* ovens and the huge piles of herbs that accompanied almost every meal – a Persian influence, no doubt. Coriander, dill, the large aniseed-flavoured

leaves of red basil, and something they called *'kress salat'* – a peppery land cress, I would imagine – were laid out on ornate brass platters. The habit must have been adopted by my dad's mum Vera, who also spent ten years in Uzbekistan, and eventually it naturally integrated into my dad's own young family's eating habits.

Years later, when I finally loved coriander (thanks to Indian and South East Asian cuisine in the UK), and realised that eating herbs whole was unusual, I started paying more attention to markets whenever I went back to Ukraine or visited Georgia. The herb displays were colossal, breathtaking, regal. Whole plants, including roots and flowers, were stacked up to the level of the vendor's chest. On top – oh, behold! – coriander with not just flowers but its young green seeds, jewels full of verdant bright flavour, embedded in its crown. A little lower, basil, equally majestic in Tyrian purple, its sceptres encrusted with little pink flowers; neat bundles of tarragon, expertly tied between two wooden sticks; dill's inside-out parasols and feathery leaves completing the entourage.

Today, I despair at the sad little supermarket bunches wrapped in plastic, and try diligently to sow my own seeds in April, and again in July. Sometimes the snails spare the plants; mostly they seem to find them as delicious as I do. To this day, the sight of whole herbs always makes me feel a mixture of ease and occasion, be it a paper plate on a picnic blanket or a golden platter next to a steaming stew.

Mango Fever
by Gurdeep Loyal

In India, there is not one mango season but many, each one crashing into the next as they avalanche from south to north. The name of each variety sings like a one-word hymn – Neelam! Alphonso! Benishan! Rajapuri! Kesar! Gulab Khas! Amrapali! Chaunsa! – each ripening in its own time and seldom blossoming with another. By April, as the hard green spheres begin to swell, a collective frenzy gathers pace, the nation united in co-dependent monitoring. Then, as if unexpectedly, those green skins sear into blisters of yellows, pinks and reds: the first mangoes drop, idolised like little plump gods.

At the season's peak in June, ripe mangoes tumble like a monsoon that spreads the frenzy across the globe, eventually falling over the streets of Southall, Tooting and Leicester, forming a trail of stacked crates that stretches all the way to Birmingham, Brick Lane and Bradford. The first sight of them ignites an annual hysteria, the nectar of mangoes holding us hostage until the season ends.

Through their embrace of June's hypnotising commotion, the Indian diaspora can appease their year-round longing for the motherland. To start with, they take to eating an entire mango to begin each day, squeezing the flesh through the swollen skins like toothpaste, then slurping their sunny oval stones in ritualistic ecstasy. Some attempt to slice the ripest mangoes into half-moon wedges for sprinkling with Kashmiri chilli, lime juice and salt; others smother ripe mangoes with more mango – dusting them with sour amchoor powder, the dried remains of unripe mangoes of seasons past.

Just as wise elders emphatically preach, yet again, that life in Britain has never tasted so sweet, it's quickly realised that one mango a day is not enough. And so mangoes become the tropical core at the heart of every meal.

The softest mangoes are added to curries and daals, their disintegrating flesh fried into sizzling pots of onions, garlic, cumin and ginger. Some mangoes are finely chopped into kachumbers: combined with raw shallots, fresh coriander, white radish and roasted peanuts, then sprinkled with mouth-puckering chaat masala to finish. Other mangoes are pulsed into creamy yellow lassis with thick yogurt, malai cream, crushed saffron and green cardamom – with flourishing drizzles of honey or condensed milk for those especially sweet-toothed.

Just before the peak of the season ends, attentions turn to mango pickling, with cauldrons of mustard oil and vinegar swiftly brewed with liberal handfuls of Himalayan salt, raw cane sugar and spices. The scalding potions are reduced to

briny amber that can defy decay, immortalising the last mangoes in preserved sanctity before the season's curtain falls.

Months later, the pickles are unearthed and unravelled from their mummified bandages. Yet what's revealed inside bears little of the ripe frenzy they vowed to conserve. Far from pausing time, the strange life inside those fermented jars has evolved in fast forward – June's mangoes now taking on extraordinary flavours completely alien to memories of the ripe fruit that once was; sweetness converted to sour, florals to salt, mellow pulp to an acid sting.

The ephemeral season has transformed into something new, just like the world outside, which now begins its invisible scheming of the next mango season that will soon come to be.

A Menu for June

by Nik Sharma

SPICED PEA SOUP

This vibrant soup is just as great enjoyed curled up on the sofa as served at a dinner party. If you have pea shoots to hand, use them to adorn each bowl. Buttered, toasted naan or bread is a must.

```
Serves 4

60g (2¼oz) ghee or unsalted butter
1 large white or yellow onion, diced
1 large carrot, trimmed, peeled and diced
1 celery stick, diced
1 tbsp peeled and grated fresh ginger
2 garlic cloves, minced
1 tsp garam masala
1 tsp Kashmiri chilli powder or ¾ tsp smoked sweet paprika and
¼ tsp cayenne pepper
300g (10oz) fresh or frozen peas (no need to thaw)
½ tsp freshly ground black pepper
Fine sea salt
1 tsp nigella seeds
1 tsp cumin seeds
Pea shoots, to garnish (optional)
```

Heat half the ghee in a large saucepan over a medium-high heat. Add the onion and sauté for about 5 minutes until translucent. Add the carrot and celery and sauté until tender and the vegetables are just starting to brown. Stir in the ginger, garlic, garam masala and chilli powder and cook until fragrant. Add the peas, along with 840ml (28fl oz) water, and bring to the boil. Cook until the peas are tender, then remove from the heat. Blitz in a blender until velvety smooth, then return the soup to the pan. Keep it simmering over a low heat. Stir in the black pepper and season with salt.

Heat the remaining ghee in a small saucepan over a medium heat. Add the nigella and cumin seeds to the hot fat; they will sizzle and turn fragrant. Remove from the heat and drizzle over the pea soup. Serve warm, garnished with fresh pea shoots alongside buttered slices of naan.

PANEER AND BEETROOT SALAD WITH MANGO-LIME DRESSING

I feel an incomparable joy that I find difficult to express in words when I eat ripe Indian mangoes. During ripening, the starch transforms and gives way to a soft pulp that's sweet and sour, carrying an aroma that reminds me of warm summer holidays in Goa. While mangoes are delicious as a sweet treat, they also make an excellent addition to savoury dishes. The fruity flavour of mangoes with lime gives this beetroot salad a refreshing taste.

```
Serves 4

400g (14oz) firm paneer, cut into 2.5 x 5cm (1 x 2in) pieces
4 beetroots (450g/1lb total weight), ideally a mixture of red and
yellow, peeled, trimmed and quartered
2 tbsp extra virgin olive oil, plus extra for greasing
Fine sea salt

For the marinade:
225ml (8fl oz) plain unsweetened kefir, buttermilk or yogurt
2 tsp fine sea salt
½ tsp ground cumin
½ tsp ground turmeric
½ tsp chilli powder
½ tsp freshly ground black pepper

For the dressing:
140g (5oz) ripe mango, diced
125ml (4fl oz) kefir or buttermilk
60ml (2fl oz) grapeseed or extra virgin olive oil
1½ tbsp fresh lime juice
1 tbsp English mustard
¼ tsp freshly ground black pepper
¼ tsp chilli powder

To serve:
200g (7oz) rocket
1 tbsp extra virgin olive oil
1 tsp freshly ground black pepper
2 tsp amchoor
```

Whisk the marinade ingredients together in a small bowl. Taste and season with more salt if needed. Pour the marinade into a large resealable bag.

Put the paneer in the bag with the marinade, seal, and gently shake to coat evenly. Leave to marinate for 1 hour at room temperature.

Preheat the oven to 200°C/400°F/gas mark 6.

Put the beetroots in a baking dish or roasting tray, drizzle with the olive oil, and season with salt. Roast for 30–45 minutes until a knife slides through the centre with ease. Remove from the oven and leave to rest for 10 minutes.

Meanwhile, prepare the dressing. Put the ingredients into a blender and pulse until combined and smooth. Taste and season with salt.

Grill the paneer just before you're ready to assemble the salad. Heat a cast-iron griddle pan or a medium non-stick frying pan over a medium-high heat and brush the surface with a little olive oil. Using a pair of kitchen tongs, carefully lift the paneer out of the bag and cook it, in batches, for 2–3 minutes on each side or until it turns golden-brown and is slightly seared.

To serve, toss the rocket in a large mixing bowl with the olive oil. Add the pepper and season with salt. Add the warm grilled paneer pieces. Drizzle with a few tablespoons of the dressing. Sprinkle with the amchoor just before serving with the remaining dressing on the side.

APRICOT, CARDAMOM AND SAFFRON CAKE

The unmistakable scent of green cardamom and delicate threads of saffron are a classic combination in Indian cooking. In this cake, fresh sun-kissed apricots are layered on top, baked and then glazed with apricot preserve. To boost the flavour, I sometimes add a pinch of cardamom and a splash of lime juice to the apricot preserve too.

Serves 12

165g (5¾oz) unsalted butter, cubed and at room temperature, plus
extra for greasing
3 large ripe but firm apricots
280g (10oz) plain flour
2 tsp baking powder
¼ tsp bicarbonate of soda
Pinch of salt
200g (7oz) caster sugar
20 saffron strands
½ tsp ground green cardamom seeds
4 large eggs, at room temperature
150g (5½oz) apricot preserve
2 tbsp boiling water

Preheat the oven to 180°C/350°F/gas mark 4. Grease a Swiss roll tin and line with baking paper, allowing it to overhang on the longer sides of the tin to help lift out the cooked cake.

Fill a medium saucepan with enough water to completely submerge the apricots and bring to a boil over a high heat. Carefully drop in the apricots and poach them for 20–30 seconds. Remove them with a slotted spoon and leave until cool enough to handle. Once cooled, peel and discard the skin; it should come off easily. Halve and stone the apricots, then slice into 6-mm (¼-in) thick wedges.

In a large bowl, dry whisk the flour, baking powder, bicarbonate of soda and salt. Put the cubed butter, sugar, saffron and cardamom in the bowl of a stand mixer. Using the paddle attachment, beat on medium speed for 3–4 minutes until the mixture is pale and fluffy. Slowly add one egg at a time, beating on a medium speed until combined, scraping down the sides and the bottom of the bowl after each addition.

Add the dry ingredients to the creamed ingredients in the stand mixer. Mix on a low speed, then beat until there are no streaks of flour visible. Transfer the batter to the prepared tin and level the surface. Layer the sliced apricots on top of the cake. Bake for 55–60 minutes, until the top is golden brown and a skewer inserted into the centre comes out clean. Remove from the oven and let the cake cool in the tin for 5 minutes before lifting out using the baking paper.

Meanwhile, prepare the glaze. Mix the apricot preserve with the boiling water in a small bowl. Brush this glaze over the surface of the warm cake.

The cake can be served warm or at room temperature. It will keep for up to four days if stored in the fridge in an airtight container.

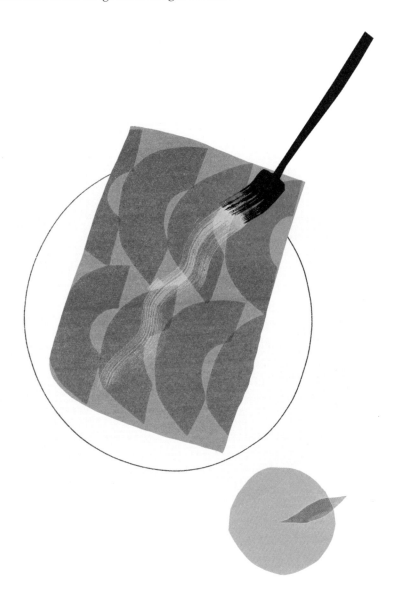

Reading List

Jane Grigson,
Jane Grigson's Vegetable Book
An alphabetical guide to vegetables interwoven with fragments of history, botany and poetry. Try the June pea soup, and pease pudding with pork. Essential reading, along with Grigson's *Fruit Book*.

Mark Diacono,
Herb
A plot-to-plate guide to getting the best from herbs, sure to inspire even the most reluctant gardener to plant a few pots. The lemon verbena limoncello is perfect for a summer's day.

Shane O'Mara,
In Praise of Walking
The latest science on how we walk and why it's good for us; persuasive enough to rouse the most ardent couch potato.

Olia Hercules,
Summer Kitchens
Recipes and reminiscences from garden kitchens across Ukraine. The preserving chapter is inspired, and the poppy seed cake is a must.

Gurdeep Loyal,
Mother Tongue
Vibrant recipes that celebrate and explore the delicious self-expression of second-generation British-Indian identity today.

Madhur Jaffrey,
Climbing the Mango Trees
An enchanting memoir of a childhood in India, from climbing mango trees armed with a mixture of salt, red chillies and roasted cumin, to enjoying picnics in the foothills of the Himalayas.

Usha Prabakaran,
Usha's Pickle Digest
A straight-talking cult classic. Ignore the questionable design and delve in for the joyous, authoritative tips and recipes for pickling everything from pea pods to mangoes to jackfruit seeds.

Nik Sharma,
The Flavor Equation
The science of great cooking intelligently explained and deliciously demonstrated through recipes, diagrams and illustrations. A book that will transform the way you cook.

July

A time to unabashedly indulge in the sweet things in life. The fields and orchards are flush with fruit, hastily ripening in the heat of high summer. Bowls of sun-warmed cherries served perfectly unadorned, classic cocktails with neon-pink garnishes, local honey harvests, pick-you-own farms and the sweet alchemy of baking peaches, pavlovas and sugar-crusted pies.

IN SEASON

Blackcurrants	Gooseberries
Blueberries	Meadowsweet
Cherries	Nasturtiums
Cherry plums	Nectarines
Courgette flowers	Pak choi
Cucumber	Peaches
French beans	Poppy seeds
Garlic	Shallots
Globe artichokes	Wild strawberries

Cherries

A brown paper bag full of plump, sun-warmed cherries might be the perfect snack on a bright summer's day – a fleeting, frivolous joy. If more than just a bag of stones make it home, chill the cherries until they're so cold and taut they burst between your teeth, releasing their carmine juices.

Wild cherry trees have grown in England since the first century, though it's possible the cherry thrived even before the Romans invaded. In the Middle Ages, great cherry fairs celebrated its arrival with drinking and dancing. Henry VIII was obsessed with the fruit, establishing orchards in Kent and bestowing the epithet 'The Garden of England' on the county. Such royal approval reinvigorated the English cherry industry, which reached its height in the 1950s. A love of cherries is so ingrained in our culture that we 'cherry-pick' our favourite things and talk about 'the cherry on top' of more than just an ice-cream sundae.

Cherries can be divided into three main types: sweet dessert cherries, sour cooking cherries, often sold as morellos, and an all-purpose hybrid known as Dukes. Look for bright, glossy cherries (they dull with age) with green stalks. Though you can cook with sweet cherries, the sour varieties have more character, making a fine cherry pie and lending a tart-sweet accent to pork and duck.

Enthusiasts may argue that there are few reasons to cook with cherries, but preserving them in sugar, vinegar or alcohol will invoke the memory of summer when the colder months set in. More immediate pleasure can be found in cakes and tarts, as well as the Limousin speciality clafoutis, traditionally made with the first ripe cherries of summer.

Almonds and cherries were made for each other – not surprising considering the stones impart a subtle bitter-almond flavour. Capture their marzipan notes in syrups and infusions, but invest in a sturdy cherry stoner for baking – it's one of the few kitchen gadgets worth buying and can be used to punch out olive stones too.

STONE COLD

Cherry stones contain small amounts of amygdalin, a bitter substance that reacts with stomach acid to form cyanide – poisonous in large amounts. However the stones can be safely used to make almond-flavoured syrup, vinegar, or cream infusions, or to add a subtle almond note to cherry jams and pies.

WHAT TO DO WITH CHERRIES

- Use the preserved cherry blossom made in April to dress fresh cherries.
- Toss a handful of stoned cherries in a salad with crisp lettuce or rocket and serve with duck or smoked ham.
- Pair with goat's cheese for an elegantly understated end to a summer lunch.
- Simmer in wine with sugar and lemon zest, and serve chilled with cream.
- Riff off the classic Black Forest gâteau or *Schwarzwälder Kirschtorte* and serve warm cherries with rich chocolate brownies.
- Eat with ricotta: on toast, in a cherry and ricotta cake, or with *papanași* – Romanian ricotta doughnuts.
- Batter and deep-fry bunches of cherries tied with thread and eat hot from the pan, sprinkled with cinnamon sugar.
- If you can find the sour variety, make Hungarian cherry soup and serve chilled for a refreshing July lunch.
- Ferment in salt for about a week to add a sweet-sour-salty edge to salads, salsas and cocktail garnishes.

MAKE AHEAD

Cherries in brandy

Simplicity itself. Tumble the cherries into a jar, add a little sugar and top with brandy. Leave for a few months, preferably until Christmas. Spoon the boozy cherries over ice cream or panna cotta and sip the fruit-flavoured brandy. Cherry vodka and gin are equally delicious.

Maraschino
by Alice Lascelles

Long before I could tell a Manhattan from a Martini, I was mesmerised by the neon-pink cocktail cherries in my parents' whiskey sours. Growing up in 1980s New York, these synthetic delicacies were everywhere – in fruit salads, on cakes, cresting cream-topped banana splits. But it was at cocktail hour that they acquired their real allure. Sometimes, if I was really lucky, a grown-up would hand their whiskey-soaked cherry to me. I'd wolf it down, delirious: a sticky, saccharine symbol of happy parents and being allowed to stay up late.

I'd like to say my palate has evolved since then – but the pleasure of eating dayglo Opies cherries hasn't diminished one bit. I still love the crunch of the plasticky skin between my teeth and the ooze of confected flesh; the sensation of twiddling the spindly pink stalk in my fingers as my mouth floods with intoxicatingly sweet almond essence, setting off all kinds of alarm bells in my brain.

I'll never say no to an Opies cherry. But the brand I most often use these days is the Italian company Luxardo. Glossy black, sweet as a Bakewell tart, but edged with a sharp acidity, they are the sombre antidote to the flamboyant Opies – not as fun, perhaps, but a far better match for booze. There is always a silver-topped, sticky-bottomed jar of them lurking somewhere in our kitchen, for putting on puddings and into drinks. I love them on ice cream, with yogurt and in cakes, but best of all when fished from the depths of a ruby-red Manhattan.

Once, when the cherry blossom was in full bloom, I paid a visit to Luxardo's home in Torreglia, in north-east Italy. I remember great wooden vats of sour marasca cherries steeping in thick sugar syrup, and squat copper pot stills bubbling away with cherry leaves, stones and twigs, to create the almondy distillate that is the backbone of Luxardo's famous maraschino liqueur. Everyone, from the pot-bellied distillers to the women weaving the raffia bottle sleeves, wore a white apron printed with the ornate Luxardo maraschino label – the same apron I now wear whenever I'm cooking at home.

I've attempted homemade cocktail cherries a few times, but I've come to the conclusion that Luxardo cherries can't be bettered. So instead, here is my take on the Aviation – a classic from the early 1900s that brings maraschino cherries *and* liqueur together in one gorgeously scented sour.

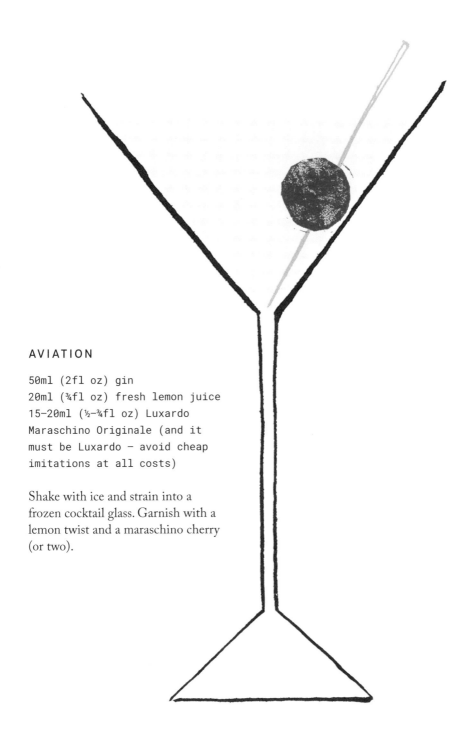

AVIATION

50ml (2fl oz) gin
20ml (¾fl oz) fresh lemon juice
15–20ml (½–¾fl oz) Luxardo
Maraschino Originale (and it
must be Luxardo — avoid cheap
imitations at all costs)

Shake with ice and strain into a
frozen cocktail glass. Garnish with a
lemon twist and a maraschino cherry
(or two).

Pick Your Own
by Anna Higham

'I have a deep compassion for our own town dwellers who know so little of fruit at its best. How many of them have ever tasted a ripe cherry, one of those that we gather on a July day, so full of juice and tender of skin that it would burst at the very sight of a bushel basket?'
The Anatomy of Dessert by Edward A. Bunyard, 1929

When I first started working in the restaurant, it was the depths of winter. I kept hearing of the pick-your-own farm we would visit every week when summer hit, my excitement building with each conversation. And for the last six summers, I have driven out to a Kentish PYO farm to pick whatever is at its best. Each visit I explore further, each year I find a new favourite tree. I initiate other chefs and friends, witnessing the revelation when they taste a strawberry so perfectly ripe, still warm from the sun, and made all the sweeter by the toil it took to find and pick it. I know they, like me, can never go back to mediocre fruit.

Kitchen work is by nature physical but stationary: endurance without flow. At the farm, I discover a new physicality – aching thighs from squatting among the strawberries, skin scratched and embedded with tiny thorns from the

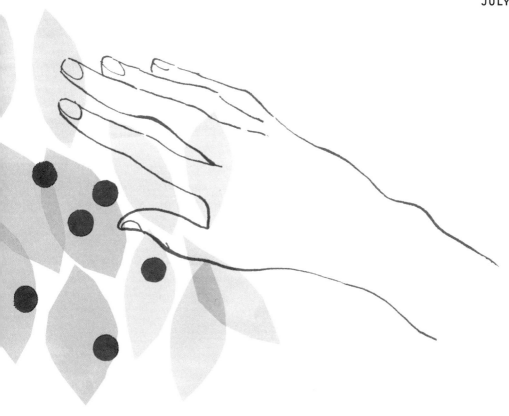

gooseberries, raspberries and tayberries. I stretch to grasp the just-out-of-reach plums. My mind finds calm in its focus of finding the next perfect fruit and my eyes see nothing but joyful colour. I always return from picking weary but somehow refreshed.

The real trick at a PYO farm is to get inside the canopy of any fruit tree or bush. Don't hover around the edges – fight your way through the branches to look out from within. Cherries are brazen, doing everything they can to be attractive, to be chosen. It's hard to keep your concentration as your eye catches yet another flash of cerise. Mulberries, on the other hand, require more patience – they hide under leaves, maintaining their mystery.

When I return to the kitchen, the need to preserve the memory of the farm takes over. I fill the cupboards with jams, compotes and cordials, and the freezer with ice creams. I'll wait until winter to prise open these sunshine jars and bottles. My belly is already full of stolen fruit, too perfectly ripe to be consumed anywhere other than within the idyll of the farm.

Honey
by Sarah Wyndham Lewis

July marks the start of summer honey harvests. Earlier crops may have been taken, but this is the crucial point in the year to assess the honey stores laid down by the bees to see them through winter's deprivations. Good beekeepers take only honey surplus to the hive's overwintering needs.

Honey is a complex wholefood. To protect its virtues, the best producers never heat their honey above hive temperature during extraction (the definition of 'raw'), never microfilter and never blend honeys from different sources.

Britain is such a densely packed island, most of our local honeys are 'polyflorals'; the product of many bee-foraged sources. Countries with more elbow room often produce 'monoflorals' – single-plant varietals from wild or cultivated sources. The word *terroir* is as meaningful to honey as it is to wine or olive oil. Rising in order of intensity, each of my preferred monoflorals listed here is as unique as a fine wine, linked through its characteristic colour, texture and flavours to the landscape where the bees labour.

LIME

Linden tree: across Europe
Fresh, bright and faintly medicinal, with an exceptional clarity of sweetness – ideal in herbal teas and gin-based honey cocktails. Lime blossom tisane with lime honey makes a perfect bedtime pairing.

LEATHERWOOD

Tasmania
Thick, buttery, wholly unforgettable, with waxy-sweet florals, camphorous notes and hints of dessert spices. Try with salty butter and oatcakes, or stir through rice pudding just before serving.

THYME

Greece, Sardinia, Sicily
Big, resinous, herby flavours elegantly parked between sweet and savoury. Partner with hard and soft cheeses as well as pork, lamb or chicken. Amplify with a sprinkle of dried thyme.

CORIANDER

Eastern Europe
Warm coriander and dill notes, a fresh,
lemony-citrus character and heady aromatics.
Blend with mustard or use to cure gravadlax.

PINE

Greece
Sensuously thick, resin-packed, powerfully
aromatic and slightly medicinal. Pair with
literally any dairy product, or just eat straight
from the jar with a large spoon.

THISTLE

Italy, Greece, Israel
Complex flavour notes including sweet florals,
warm caramels, green herbs, cinnamon and
bitter almonds. Plays well against nuts, hard
goat's cheeses and fruity olive oils.

BUCKWHEAT

France, Eastern Europe
A lamb in wolf's clothing, with none of the
pronounced sweetness of most honeys. Get over its
'zoo' nose and explore heavenly flavours of blackcurrant
and malt tending towards savoury. Try with blue cheese
or with soured cream on blinis.

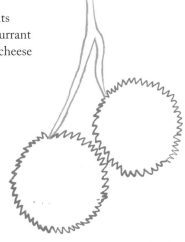

ARBUTUS

Sardinia
Scarily bitter on first approach, blooming into
lush coffee, vanilla and floral notes. Famous since
classical times as '*miele amaro*' and traditionally eaten
with young goat's or sheep's cheeses and walnuts.

Sweet Alchemy
by Deborah Levy

Honey is alchemy, medicine, poetry. Somewhere in the world right now, a honey bee is sucking nectar from flowers, dazed, satiated, purposeful. When this precious little bee is full, it returns to the hive. We won't go into the dominatrix queen and her loyal drones here, but the delicate ecosystem that produces honey is the alchemy and poetry of which I speak – the transformation of one thing into another.

In cities choked with traffic and where ravenous foxes scavenge for junk food tossed on pavements, the honey we store in our kitchen cupboards brings us closer to an elsewhere of orange blossom or pine trees, clover, lavender, carob. Honey is also time. It is possible that many generations of bees are involved in the production of a single jar. In this regard, perhaps honey is the one consistent food that has followed me from childhood to adulthood – a substitute for the loss of a loving parental presence, sweet as a kiss, as cloying and suffocating as the rules that maddened us as teenagers.

Hippocrates, the ancient Greek father of medicine, who understood that disease was not the revenge of wrathful gods, suggested that honey could soften lip ulcers and help heal running sores. During the pandemic, I made big pots of pestled fresh turmeric and licorice root mixed with lemon juice and spoonfuls of thick thyme honey. I encouraged my daughters to drink this witchy brew, probably because it made me feel less helpless, but I secretly believed it to be protective. I also tried to make mead, that ancient wine known as the nectar of the gods, its main ingredients being raw honey, spring water and champagne yeast. This went so badly wrong that I was reminded honey was also used to preserve and embalm bodies.

Of all the fruit on display in high summer, I most look forward to the adventure of apricots. I like to roast them in the oven, cut in half, leaving in the stones to hold them together. Their pulp becomes more intense in colour and flavour as they bake. I sometimes add a squeeze of orange juice, and prefer to eat the fruit cold, ladled with orange blossom honey, a handful of burnt almonds and sometimes even a dash of peppery olive oil. Other times, I have added a splash of sweet amaretto liqueur, but have decided it tends to take over the flavour, like someone hogging the conversation.

I tasted a finessed version of this dish one summer in Paris – a sort of trifle made only from baked apricots harvested in the south of France. It was presented in a glass, the orange flesh layered with almonds, dark wildflower honey and a small, perfect amount of thick Normandy cream. Sitting at that table under the shade of a tree, dazed and satiated, I watched as blossom fell in slow motion on the hot cobblestones.

A Menu for July
by Ravneet Gill

When friends are coming over or a summer party is planned, it's always nice to have a few options that really showcase seasonal fruit in all its glory. Here are three sweet recipes that often grace my table – and always disappear very quickly.

STRAWBERRY, ALMOND AND HONEY PAVLOVA

Serves 6-8

4 egg whites
1 tbsp white wine vinegar
1 tbsp vanilla bean paste or extract
200g (7oz) caster sugar
2 tbsp cornflour
300ml (10fl oz) double cream
1 tbsp runny honey, plus extra for drizzling
Pinch of sea salt
300g (10½oz) strawberries, hulled and halved
60g (2¼oz) skin-on, roasted almonds, chopped
A few thyme sprigs, leaves picked

Preheat the oven to 100°C/gas mark ¼ and line a baking sheet with baking paper.

In a stand mixer, whisk together the egg whites, vinegar and vanilla on medium speed for 7–10 minutes, past the frothy stage, until you see soft peaks form. Start adding the sugar a tablespoon at a time, gradually increasing the speed as you do so. Continue whisking for 2–3 minutes until stiff peaks form and the meringue is thick and glossy.

Add the cornflour, mixing slowly at first and gradually increasing the speed until it is incorporated. Stop here – you don't want the meringue to deflate.

Shape the meringue into a large disc on your prepared baking sheet and bake for 2–3 hours. You will know it's done when you can lift it cleanly from the paper. Remove the meringue from the oven and leave it to cool completely.

To serve, lightly whip the cream with the honey and salt until it holds its shape. Top the meringue with the cream, strawberries and roasted almonds, then finish with a drizzle of honey and some picked thyme leaves.

ROASTED PEACHES, MASCARPONE AND GRAHAM CRACKER CRUMB

Serves 4

4 large ripe peaches
Zest and juice of 1 orange
2 tbsp soft light brown sugar
250g (9oz) mascarpone
2 heaped tbsp icing sugar
Pinch of sea salt

For the crumb:
160g (5¾oz) plain flour
25g (1oz) caster sugar
25g (1oz) dark brown sugar
¼ tsp ground cinnamon
¼ tsp ground ginger
¼ tsp fine sea salt
¼ tsp bicarbonate of soda
115g (4oz) unsalted butter, cubed
40g (1½oz) golden syrup or honey

Preheat the oven to 160°C/325°F/gas mark 3.

To make the crumb, put the flour, sugars, spices, salt and bicarbonate into a bowl and mix. Add the butter and rub between your fingers until the mixture has a breadcrumb consistency. Then add the golden syrup or honey and mix until a dough forms. Break this mixture up into small pieces and place on a baking tray. Bake for 25–35 minutes until golden. Remove from the oven and allow to cool before blitzing. Keep the oven on for roasting the peaches.

Cut the peaches in half (keep the stones in one half) and toss them in a bowl with half of the orange juice and the brown sugar. Arrange the peaches in a shallow baking dish, skin-side up. Bake for 15–20 minutes or until they are soft to the touch and the skin has blistered slightly. Allow to cool for 5 minutes before removing the skins by gently pulling them away from the flesh of the peach – this should be easy to do. If not, they may need longer in the oven.

Meanwhile, in a large bowl, gently beat the mascarpone until soft. Add the icing sugar, salt, orange zest and the remaining orange juice. Mix well, being careful not to let the mascarpone split.

Remove the stones and serve the peaches warm with the mascarpone dolloped on the side and the crumb scattered over the top.

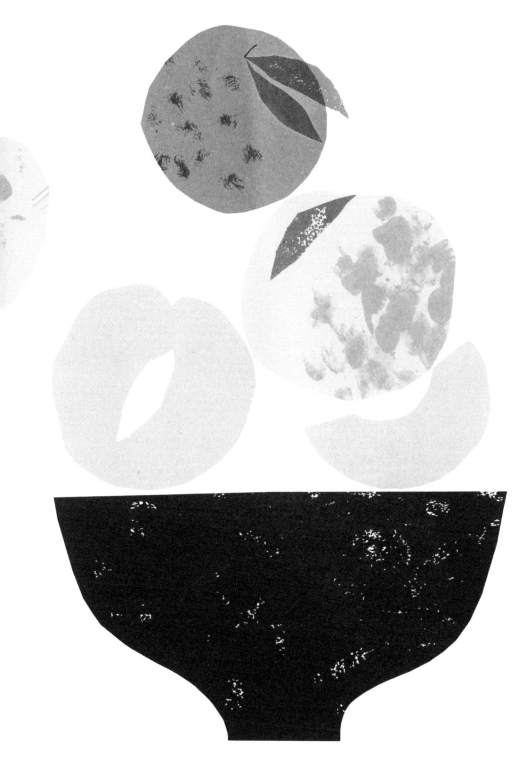

CHERRY PIE

Serves 6-8

For the pastry:
225g (8oz) strong white flour
5g (⅛oz) fine salt
15g (½oz) caster sugar
175g (6oz) unsalted butter,
cold, cubed
70ml (2½fl oz) ice-cold water
2 tbsp milk
1 tbsp demerara sugar

For the filling:
500g (1lb 2oz) stoned cherries
180g (6¼oz) golden caster sugar
50g (1¾oz) cornflour
¼ tsp almond extract or
Disaronno

In a large bowl, or the bowl of a stand mixer, mix together the flour, salt and caster sugar. Add the butter and mix until the mixture resembles breadcrumbs – you still want to be able to see some chunks of butter. Add the water in one go and mix quickly to form a dough. Tip the dough onto your work surface and bring together with your hands. Cover and place in the fridge to firm up for about 4 hours.

To make the filling, coat the cherries in the sugar, cornflour and almond extract or Disaronno. Set aside while you prepare the pie case. Some juice may leach from the cherries, but don't worry too much, that's where the cornflour will help.

Remove the dough from the fridge and gently knead it on a lightly floured surface. Cut off a third and set aside for the top. Roll out the rest to 4mm (¼in) thick. Grease a 20cm (8in) tart tin or a solid-based cake tin. Line the tin with the pastry, leaving a bit of an overhang. Add any scraps of pastry to the reserved dough. Put the lined tin in the fridge to chill.

Roll out the rest of the pastry to 4mm (¼in) thick and either cut a lattice or leave whole, then chill for 15 minutes on a tray lined with baking paper.

Once the case and top are cold, put the cherries into the tart case, cover and pinch the pastry edges together to seal the lid. If you have left it whole, pierce a hole in the middle. Return to the fridge.

Preheat the oven to 200°C/400°F/gas mark 6. Put a heavy baking tray in the oven to heat up – it works best on the bottom shelf.

Brush the top of the pie with the milk and sprinkle with the demerara sugar. Bake on the tray for 1 hour 15 minutes until golden brown. Allow to cool slightly before serving with ice cream, custard or cream – or all three!

Reading List

Alan Major,
Cherries in the Rise
An in-depth look at the cultivation of cherries in Kent through the centuries.

Alice Lascelles,
Ten Cocktails
A stylish and witty account of ten classic cocktails, with stories, recipes and tips on the convivial art of drinking.

Anna Higham,
The Last Bite
Dessert recipes that move through the year fruit by fruit, ingredient by ingredient, starting with the first strawberries of summer and ending with the new blossoms and herbs of spring.

Sarah Wyndham Lewis,
Planting for Honeybees
Practical advice on how to help bees flourish by creating a habitat for them no matter how small or large your space – from a window ledge in the city to a country garden.

Hattie Ellis,
Spoonfuls of Honey
A guide to the varieties and flavours of nature's sweetest gift, from manuka in New Zealand to heather in Scotland, alongside recipes for sweet and savoury honey dishes.

Deborah Levy,
Swimming Home
A sharp and thrilling novel set in the south of France and a haunting exploration of loss and longing.

Ravneet Gill,
Sugar, I Love You
Knockout recipes that celebrate the sweeter things in life: cheesecakes from around the world, sweet doughs such as Devonshire splits and Danish *brunsviger*, cookies, waffles and classic ring doughnuts.

August

A month of abundance, both in spirit and on the plate. Indulge in preposterous ice cream sundaes piled high in pretty glasses; sweet smiles of melon eaten swiftly and hungrily; voluptuous tomatoes seasoned only with salt; and the smoky char of summertime barbecues. Harness the heat of fresh chillies – whether in sambals or salsas – to transform everyday meals, inspired by faraway places where summer is less fleeting.

IN SEASON

Aubergine
Broccoli
Bilberries
Courgette
Fennel
Loganberries
Marsh samphire
Melons
Mulberries

Redcurrants
Rowan
Runner beans
Scented geraniums
Summer truffles
Tomatoes
Tomatillos
Whitecurrants

Tomatoes

SOME LIKE IT HOT

Tomatoes are the colour of love and lust, their voluptuous contours and ripe juiciness providing pleasure on the palate and the plate. Though they prefer the heat of southern climes, we're unable to resist their allure, racing to ripen the fruit during our short summers. Yet our love for tomatoes hasn't always been unconditional. When tomatoes arrived in Europe from South America in the 1520s, they came burdened with reputations for being ornamental, herbal and even toxic. It took 200 years for their culinary possibilities to be appreciated, slowly migrating from our gardens to our kitchens.

Tomatoes at their peak need only olive oil and salt to let their natural acidity shine. Look for tomatoes with character – bulbous and misshapen, with folds and creases, furrows and cracks. The best will feel heavy for their size, sweet and tart with firm flesh. Keep them in the fruit bowl in a sunny spot to make them feel at home.

Tomatoes and bread have long been bedfellows. Thick slices on good bread, buttered with a heavy hand, makes a satisfying lunch. To avoid repetition, alternate with garlic-spiked *pan con tomate*, grating fat tomatoes to a fresh pulp and letting it soften crisp toasted bread just the right amount; or layer up a *pan bagnat*, essentially a niçoise salad in a bun. Their versatility is never-ending, but their intensity often benefits from the calming blandness of carbs.

Grilling or roasting tomatoes deepens their flavour – a simple gratin sprinkled with garlic, parsley and breadcrumbs is quick enough for summer cooking. When the temperature rises, blitz ripe tomatoes and ice to a cool, smooth soup, reserving a little of the juice to make fresh Bloody Marys. Wait until the weather cools for stews, sauces, curries and soups, and switch to canned tomatoes in winter to avoid disappointment. Tomatoes need sunshine, even when they've journeyed far from their ancestral home.

THE LOOK OF LOVE

In the 1550s, tomatoes were given the name *pomi d'oro* or 'golden apple' by the Venetian herbalist Pietro Andrea Matthioli, a phrase that survives in the Italian word *pomodoro*. Some believed tomatoes were an aphrodisiac, despite suspicions that they were poisonous, and so they came to England as the 'apple of love' or 'love-apple', an idiom that lingered long into the nineteenth century.

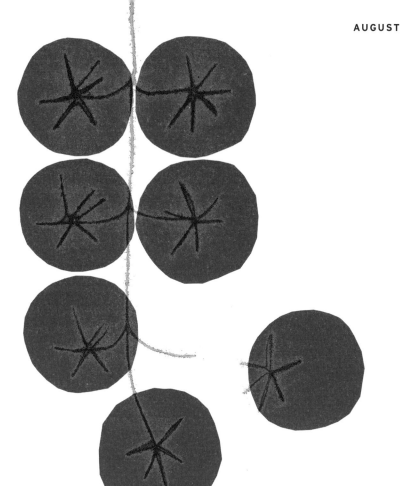

MAKE AHEAD

Tomato leaves

The heady herbal aroma of tomato leaves can be used to add depth and intrigue to tomato dishes: add to a simmering tomato sauce, dry and fold into pizza dough, infuse in olive oil or add a handful to your favourite pesto. Lillie O'Brien recommends using the leaves and stems in jam, boiling them up with the fruit and adding a few to the sugar first to intensify the flavour. Try her plum and tomato leaf jam from *Five Seasons of Jam* when the first purple plums arrive.

The Power of Sambal

by Lara Lee

Sharing food is an act of love, one that grounds us and brings us comfort. We often yearn for the food that reminds us of a moment in time, of family, of place. For me, and many Indonesians who crave the food that reminds them of home, that comfort is sambal.

This spicy, hot condiment has chilli as its star ingredient, though you will find vastly different sambals depending on which region you visit in Indonesia, as diverse as the natural landscape that stretches across the 17,500 islands. It may be raw or cooked, chopped or ground into a paste, made with fresh or dried ingredients. What is consistent is that sambal sits at the heart of every meal, served alongside rice, vegetables, fish or meat and *kerupuk*, an Indonesian cracker that stimulates the appetite. Sambal exists to complement food, rather than overpower it, and Indonesians will eat a little sambal with every bite; no meal is complete without it.

Sambal originated on the island of Java, and historical Indonesian texts record 352 different kinds. That figure doesn't include the thousands of unofficial variations throughout the country, where every home cook proudly boasts their family recipe 'is better than yours'. In its simplest form, you will find *sambal ulek*, where boiled, ground red chillies are combined with salt, oil and sometimes a little vinegar.

In west Sumatra, *sambal hijau Padang* is made from caramelised ground green chillies perfumed with lime leaf, citrus, garlic, shallots and crispy fried anchovies. Travel further east to the Hindu island of Bali, and *sambal matah* is served sliced and raw with lemongrass, chillies and garlic coated in lime and hot oil. Indonesia's national motto, *bhinneka tunggal ika*, translates as 'out of many, one' which means unity in diversity. From a culinary standpoint, what unites them all is sambal.

I was introduced to sambal from a young age when Popo, my grandmother, relocated from Kupang in Timor to live with in Australia, bringing her recipes to our table. The taste of her sambal was too hot for a five-year-old's tender palate, but its presence symbolised a cherished moment I looked forward to every day: our family dinner. My father worked two jobs to support us and dinner was the only time I got to see him. The dishes changed daily, but always standing proud at the centre of the table was Popo's sambal, radiant and scarlet, the colour of blood and fire, a constant reminder of that precious hour at home together.

Food offers passage to the past. Eating sambal, I see Popo's brown and wrinkled hands rhythmically grinding the ingredients down to a paste; I hear her wok sizzle as the sambal caramelises in shimmering oil, the burning sting of chilli filling the air. For me, and many Indonesians who are far from the tropical isles of their motherland, sambal has the power to transport us, to provide escape in that brief moment when its piquant heat dances on our tongues.

SAMBAL BAJAK

The joy of sambal comes from its ability to transform any meal into a triumph. In my kitchen, I'll add a spoonful of sambal next to scrambled eggs for breakfast, or drizzle it over a takeaway pizza. I simply cannot eat *nasi goreng* (fried rice) or *mie goreng* (fried noodles) without it, and a generous dollop will always be plonked into the centre of *soto ayam* (fragrant chicken soup).

The addition of tomatoes gives this East Javanese sambal its umami-rich flavour, balanced by the sourness of tamarind and the sultry heat of the chillies. *Bajak* is the Javanese word for plough, and legend states that *sambal bajak* was brought daily to farmers working in the rice fields. The heat levels of sambals vary, but this one is traditionally less spicy to aid the farmers' digestion, which is why I've used large, deseeded chillies. Perfumed with lime leaf and lemongrass, the fragrance is meant to stimulate the appetite to encourage the farmers to eat more, so they have the energy to finish the day's work.

4 tbsp neutral vegetable oil, such as sunflower
12 long red chillies (about 150g/5½oz), deseeded and sliced
3 small banana shallots or 6 Thai shallots, sliced
2 garlic cloves, sliced
150g tomatoes, quartered
1 lime leaf
1 lemongrass stalk, bruised
1 tsp tamarind paste
Palm or brown sugar, to taste
Sea salt and freshly ground black pepper

Heat half the oil in a frying pan or wok over a medium heat. Add the chillies, shallots and garlic and fry for about 5 minutes, moving the ingredients around the pan continuously so they do not burn, then remove from the heat. Transfer to a food processor, along with the tomatoes, and blend to a semi-coarse paste.

Return the pan to a medium heat and add the remaining oil. Return the spice paste to the pan and add the lime leaf and lemongrass. Continue to cook the sambal for a further 10–15 minutes, then season with the tamarind, sugar, salt and pepper before serving. Sambal will keep for up to a week in the fridge in a sealed container and for three months in the freezer.

The Ice-Cream Van

by Megan Nolan

I once dated a man who refused to believe there was such a thing as a butter and sugar sandwich, that growing up I was offered one by my little neighbour, that we ate it on a trip to the beach, with the sand crunching interchangeably with the sweet grains of sugar. The man, because his family was wealthy (which he considered to be normal), thought it sounded too idyllically impoverished. He thought that I was exaggerating the depths of my childhood hardship for effect, that my fond recollection of these sandwiches was like an Enid Blyton story about kids on a council estate.

The place where I was born and lived during my early childhood was known by those who didn't live there to be rough and violent (it was memorably once described by a newspaper as one of Ireland's 'Hell Estates'), but I mostly don't remember it that way. What I remember best is ice cream; specifically, those vulgar beasts called Screwballs. Screwballs are plastic cones filled with cheap ice cream and concluding with what back then appeared to be a fiercely substantial gumball. We buzzed happily outside the ice-cream van parked on the kerb of the green which formed the centre point of our square and therefore our world. We pushed one another and skipped the queue, and my brothers pulled me along in a tricycle wagon.

The ice cream in a Screwball was sometimes a comparatively tasteful raspberry ripple, and sometimes an unforgettable vivid blue, which is what I see now. Blue handprints and tongues and hair and the charmingly disgusting sort of sharing unique to childhood; one brother getting a go on the bubblegum first and softening it out, the other allowed the first full chew, then passed down to me for lasts like a pre-digested worm to a baby bird. The rush of chemical flavouring, the drive of pure sugar lust when I pushed my nose right into the cone to search out the last of it. Greed, but communal greed.

What remains now of my early life are not the stories about drug dealers and burnt-out cars, which despite their proximity never materially touched my childhood. Instead, I am left with the memories of automatic, careless sharing. The feeling – which does not so often exist in the area where I live now, nor in this period of my life – that things were literally made to be passed around, that they would lose their meaning if everyone didn't have a go.

This is still what ice cream is to me now. My friend and I on a trip to Milan conspiring that I will get the pistachio and she the honeycomb flavour so that we can swap halfway through. Introducing my boyfriend to some of my closest people for the first time, we gather after dinner around a bowl of green pea ice cream with chocolate soil, five spoons working into the masterpiece at once. And he, trying to soothe me during my all-time worst hangover, bringing to our bed a bowl of birthday cake-flavoured ice cream. He apologises for the unsophisticated flavour, saying it was all they had, but it's perfect because it tastes synthetic like the shared treats of my youth, and I slurp at it tentatively beneath the covers, whole again.

Knickerbocker Glory
by Terri Mercieca

A classic ice-cream sundae with retro vibes and luxurious layers, the knickerbocker glory has graced the tables of British seaside towns since the 1920s. It has everything you want in a nostalgic dessert: a ridiculous name, a tower of ice cream and fruity sauce, a magnificent swoosh of whipped cream and a fan wafer to top it off – oh, and a cherry of course!

I don't think I'm going too much against tradition by adding a little pizzazz here with one of my favourite flavour combinations: strawberry and popcorn. I used to be sceptical about no-churn ice cream, but I was wrong. This recipe is easy enough to make at home without an ice-cream machine. Go wild with extra embellishments, be they sprinkles, gold leaf, wafer cigars or, my personal favourite, a cocktail umbrella. This is already a preposterously elaborate dessert, it's impossible to take it too far.

STRAWBERRY POPCORN KNICKERBOCKER GLORY

Serves 6, with leftover ice cream for rainy days

Popcorn ice cream

For the no-churn ice cream:
1 litre (2 pints) double cream
400g (14oz) condensed milk
20g (½oz) freeze-dried corn powder (optional)

For the salted butter popcorn:
4 tsp sunflower oil
250g (9oz) popping corn
25g (1oz) unsalted butter, melted
Pinch of sea salt

For the caramel popcorn:
200g (7oz) caster sugar
60g (2¼oz) freshly popped corn (reserved from the amount above)
50g (1¾oz) unsalted butter

First make the butter popcorn. Heat the oil in a large, heavy-based saucepan with a tight-fitting lid over a medium–high heat. Once the oil is hot, drop in one kernel and put the lid on. When it pops, add the rest of the popping corn and quickly put the lid back on. Lower the heat to medium and shake the pan occasionally so the popcorn doesn't burn on the bottom. When it sounds as if all the kernels have popped, remove from the heat and wait for any stragglers to pop. Carefully lift the lid and remove 60g (2¼oz) for the caramel popcorn, then add the butter and salt to the pan and shake it to coat each piece. Leave to cool, then pick out any unpopped kernels and discard.

Gently heat the double cream in another lidded pan over a low heat. Just before it boils, add the salted butter popcorn, then put the lid on and put the pan straight in the fridge to infuse. Leave the mixture to cool to 10°C (50°F). Using a stick blender, blitz until the popcorn is reduced to smaller pieces, but not a purée; this is just to draw out more flavour. Pass the mixture through a sieve into a bowl, pressing down on the soggy popcorn to remove as much liquid as possible. Add the condensed milk and corn powder to the flavoured cream. Blend until smooth. Return to the fridge for a few hours until it has cooled to 4°C (39°F) or leave overnight. Put a 1.5-litre (2¾-pint) ice-cream container in the fridge to chill.

Meanwhile, make the caramel popcorn using the reserved popped corn. Line a baking tray with baking paper. Clean and dry the large pan used for the salted popcorn and place over a medium heat. When the base smokes a little, add a quarter of the sugar and allow to caramelise. Once it is liquid and a little darker in colour than honey, stir in another quarter. Repeat until all the sugar is caramelised. It's key not to make the caramel dark too soon or it will taste bitter. Continue cooking until it is a deep-brown colour. Look for small bubbles, good colour and a little smoke, then carefully add the butter. Swirl the pan, turn off the heat and add the reserved popcorn. Continue to stir until each piece is coated in caramel and all the butter has melted. Tip onto the lined tray and separate the pieces. Leave to cool and set. Reserve about half of the best popcorn pieces for layering and decoration, and blitz the rest to a fine powder.

Remove the chilled cream mixture from the fridge and whisk until soft peaks form. Spoon half into the chilled container, sprinkle with half of the caramel popcorn powder, then add the rest of the cream mixture and sprinkle the remaining powder on top. Freeze overnight, or for at least 4 hours.

Macerated strawberries

```
200g (7oz) strawberries, hulled
Golden caster sugar (5 per cent of the weight of the hulled fruit)
```

Slice the strawberries, sprinkle with sugar and leave somewhere warm for the sugar to draw out their moisture. Reserve half for layering the knickerbocker glory and purée the other half in a blender to make a sauce.

Chantilly cream

```
600ml (1¼ pints) double cream
30g (1oz) golden caster sugar
Seeds from 2 vanilla pods (or 1 tsp best-quality vanilla paste)
Micro pinch of sea salt
```

Put all the ingredients in a bowl and whisk until firm peaks form. This is the topping, so we want it to hold a glorious peak above the glass and be able to decorate it with popcorn and strawberries.

Assembly

Pre-chill your glasses, preferably tall sundae ones: this needs to be over the top. I usually draw a plan of how I want to layer my dessert, but you can freestyle.

First, place a scoop of the ice cream in the base of each glass. Cover with some macerated berries, ensuring you allow enough for all the glasses and several layers. Trickle some sauce over the fruit and around the edge of the glass – you want to create the famous knickerbocker-glory stripes. Next, add a layer of caramel popcorn. Repeat twice, and that should take you to the top of the glass.

Pipe or dollop enough Chantilly cream on top so that it sits above the glass like a cream mountain and decorate with the remaining caramel popcorn and strawberries. Serve immediately.

A Menu for August
by Thomasina Miers

WARM CORN SALAD WITH A TOUCH OF SPICE

A simple but delicious salad that's one of my favourite ways to use late summer corn. The sweetness of the corn is laced with warmth from the spices and the final sprinkling of smoked paprika, enlivened by the fresh herbs and lime. It makes an elegant starter with tostadas or a great side dish for an al fresco lunch.

Serves 4–6

4 corn on the cob
A slug of olive oil and a knob of butter
1 onion, finely chopped
1 green chilli, finely chopped
2 garlic cloves, chopped
A few good pinches each of ground allspice and cinnamon
Juice of 1–2 limes
Handful of chopped coriander and tarragon leaves
Sea salt and freshly ground black pepper

To serve:
Soured cream
Grated pecorino or Parmesan
Pinch of hot smoked paprika
Warm flatbreads or corn tostadas

Working over a bowl, scrape a knife down each cob, held at a 45-degree angle to shave off the kernels.

Heat the oil and butter in a frying pan over a medium heat and, when it is gently sizzling, add the onion, corn and chilli. Cook for at least 5 minutes, or until the onion has turned translucent without colouring, before adding the garlic, spices, salt and pepper. Turn up the heat and cook for a further 5–10 minutes until the corn starts gently taking on some colour and caramelising.

Squeeze over the lime juice, scatter with the fresh herbs and serve on small plates with generous spoonfuls of soured cream, a little grated cheese and a pinch of paprika. Eat with warm flatbreads or corn tostadas.

TLAYUDAS

There are two streets in Oaxaca City in southern Mexico where you can find *tlayudas* made for the late-night revellers crawling out of *cantinas*, *mezcalerias* and salsa bars. The originals are made with *masa harina* (corn flour), but I find it hard to get the texture right with the type available here, so instead I use spelt flour or experiment with the amazing range of low gluten varieties that are now in all the shops. I like to cook these straight over the charcoal of a barbecue, just as they do in Mexico – don't be afraid to let the dough char a little.

Makes 5–6

250g (9oz) white spelt flour, plus extra for dusting
½ tsp baking powder
½ tsp salt
60g (2¼oz) butter, at room temperature
190ml (scant 7fl oz) yogurt or buttermilk

Combine the dry ingredients in a bowl and rub in the butter with your fingertips until you have a scruffy, scraggy dough. Add the yogurt and knead for about 2–3 minutes. Cover the bowl with a tea towel and rest for 30 minutes.

Lightly flour your work surface and divide the mixture into 80g (2¾oz) balls, covering them with a damp cloth as you go. Roll out each one on the floured surface, trying to make them as thin as you can, to about 20cm (8in) diameter.

You can cook these tlayudas on the barbecue, in a pizza oven, on a griddle pan or in a dry frying pan. Toast them for about 30 seconds until they puff up, then flip and cook for another 30 seconds on the other side. Put each one onto a hot plate and cover with a tea towel while you cook the rest.

Two favourite toppings for tlayudas:

Courgettes, courgette flowers, chervil and pecorino

For each tlayuda, shave ½ courgette (yellow or green) with a peeler to get long, thin strips. Place on top of the tlayuda with 25g (1oz) pecorino and 50g (1¾oz) mozzarella and strew with chervil and, if available, some torn courgette flowers. Season well with salt, pepper and a drizzle of truffle oil, should you have any.

Sobrasada, avocado, rocket and pecorino

Sobrasada is a spreadable cooking chorizo, but if you can't get hold of it, use slices of ordinary cured chorizo. Scatter each tlayuda with 25g (1oz) grated pecorino and 25g (1oz) grated Parmesan, then drizzle with 25g (1oz) sobrasada (warmed in a small pan). Season well and grill. Top with avocado and rocket.

MEXICAN FLANS WITH MEZCAL RASPBERRIES

Rich, velvety vanilla cream, burnt caramel, smoky mezcal and zesty lime raspberries... this is a wonderful finish to a summer dinner.

```
Makes 8

4 large eggs plus 1 yolk
150g (5½oz) caster sugar
500ml (18fl oz) double cream
350ml (12fl oz) whole milk
1 tsp vanilla extract

For the caramel:
200g (7oz) caster sugar
1-2 tbsp mezcal

For the raspberries:
300g (10½oz) raspberries
30g (1oz) caster sugar
1-2 tbsp mezcal
Zest and juice of 1-2 limes
```

First make the caramel. Heat the sugar and 3 tablespoons water in a heavy-based pan over a medium heat. Carefully melt the sugar, without stirring, then increase the heat. Let the sugar simmer gently and allow to caramelise, swirling the pan to distribute the sugar evenly as patches darken in colour. It will take around 10–12 minutes, depending on the heat; it should be a deep maple-brown colour and smell delicious. When the caramel looks right, turn the heat right down, then carefully pour in the mezcal and 1 tablespoon water and whisk until the caramel is smooth. Divide the caramel between 8 dariole moulds and set aside somewhere cool to set.

Preheat the oven to 150°C/300°F/gas mark 2.

To make the flans, whisk the eggs, extra yolk and sugar together in a large bowl until the sugar dissolves, then whisk in the cream, milk and vanilla extract. Put the moulds in a deep-sided baking tray and fill each with about 150ml (5fl oz) of the mixture. Put the tray in the oven and fill with enough boiling water to come halfway up the outside of the moulds. Bake for 40–45 minutes or until just set. The flans will wobble gently but they should hold their shape – they will continue setting in the fridge later. Remove from the oven and cool for 30 minutes before refrigerating for at least 4 hours or overnight.

When you are ready to serve, toss the raspberries in the sugar, mezcal and lime zest and juice. Turn out each flan onto a small plate and serve with some raspberries on the side.

Reading List

Clarissa Hyman,
Tomato: A Global History
The juicy history of an everyday
ingredient, from its ancestral home in
Mesoamerica to the future of tomato
genetics.

Lara Lee,
Coconut and Sambal
A heartfelt homage to the culinary
heritage of Indonesia, with recipes
from across the archipelago alongside
the fragrant, spicy sambals that are
undoubtedly the heart and soul of
every meal.

Megan Nolan,
Acts of Desperation
A fearless debut novel about obsessive
love and the dark turns it can take.

Caroline and Robin Weir,
Ice creams, Sorbets and Gelati
The definitive guide to frozen desserts,
with hundreds of recipes alongside the
history and science of ice-cream making.

Thomasina Miers,
Home Cook
An inspiring guide to enjoying good
food any day of the week. Every
recipe includes a follow-up meal idea
so that ingredients or sauces can be
ingeniously repurposed.

Sybille Bedford,
A Visit to Don Otavio
A captivating memoir of travelling in
Mexico after the Second World War,
from the evocative food scenes to the
titular visit to Don Otavio, a young
and otherworldly Mexican from a
bankrupt aristocratic family.

September

September is full of possibilities, the seasons colliding in a spectacular show of fruits and vegetables. Gaudy reds turn to deep purple – figs and plums and fingers stained with wild berries gathered on countryside walks. Forage along the coast for sea vegetables, search the hedgerows, and gather gluts from the veg patch – then return to the kitchen to preserve the bounty for colder months to come.

IN SEASON

Blackberries
Bullaces
Chanterelles
Chard
Chillies
Cobnuts
Crab apples
Damsons
Elderberries

Figs
Greengages
Hazelnuts
Lingonberries
Marrow
Peppers
Plums
Sea Buckthorn
Sweetcorn

Sea Buckthorn

Bright orange berries appear along wind-whipped scrub and sand dunes in early autumn, a feast for the birds and a curious elixir for our tables. Native to the British Isles, sea buckthorn has occupied our coastlines for millennia, yet our knowledge of these nutrient-rich berries has been all but lost.

Legend has it the mythical winged horse Pegasus descended from the heavens to eat these seaberries, giving him the power to fly. So begins a long history of myth and medicine that follows the trail of the most inhospitable landscapes, from the high altitude of the Himalayas to the tundra of Mongolia. Sea buckthorn can tolerate extreme cold, the tangle of roots knotting together the poorest of soils. The British seaside must seem like a balmy holiday, even in the depths of winter.

Look for narrow, silvery leaves and clusters of neon berries when foraging for sea buckthorn (the berries can also be bought online, frozen or pressed into juice). Wear thick gloves and pick with care – the berries burst easily and there are sharp thorns along the woody stems. It's easier to cut whole branches – the shrubs grow vigorously and benefit from a bit of forager's pruning – and freeze them so the berries hold their shape as you pull or shake them from the stem. Don't be tempted to pop one in your mouth to taste: eaten raw, they are unbelievably sour.

Tart with a sherbet tang, the flavour of sea buckthorn is akin to passion fruit mixed with citrus. Gently cook the berries to release the juices, then push through a sieve or squeeze through muslin. The juice keeps well due to its high acidity (or you can freeze it if you've made a big batch), and can be mixed with sweeter juices, sugar, honey or maple syrup. Take it as a daily tonic to ward off colds (it's incredibly high in vitamin C, minerals and omegas), use it like a cordial, or add a dash to sparkling wine for a Sea Buck's Fizz.

Unsweetened, the juice can replace lemons, adding a citrus zing to salads and fish. Infuse the berries in vinegar for dressings, or bubble them up into a jelly with apples and serve with game. Rick Stein swaps orange for sea buckthorn in a duck dish spiced with chilli, ginger and star anise, where its sharp acidity cuts through the rich meat. But if you add enough sugar, sea buckthorn sings in desserts, whipped up in creams, syllabubs and dark chocolate mousse.

MAKE AHEAD

Pickled chillies

Chillies are one of the easiest vegetables to grow, as happy on a sunny windowsill as in the garden or allotment. If you have a glut, simply squeeze as many as possible into a sterilised jar and top with pickling liquor – or hang them up to dry to make your own dried chillies, and therefore your own chilli oil, perfect for drizzling on pizza. If you can find fresh jalapeños, their milder flavour makes a particularly useful pickle: add to tacos, nachos, salsas and cornbread.

Sea Vegetables
by Darina Allen

For thousands of years, coastal communities around the world have foraged for seaweeds, shellfish and myriad sea vegetables, the collective name given to plants and algae in or near the sea. Here in Ireland, we are favoured by nature, with more than 600 edible seaweed varieties around our coast.

The popularity of seaweed was waning up until relatively recently, but interest has been rekindled by the realisation that sea vegetables are the most nutrient-dense foods on the planet, with infinitely more minerals, vitamins and trace elements than anything grown on land. Creative cooks and chefs have begun to incorporate raw, pickled and dried seaweeds into their menus, as Myrtle Allen had been doing at Ballymaloe House since it opened in 1964.

At a time when concern is mounting about the diminishing fertility of the soil, sea vegetables can fill the nutritional gap. They also play an important role in helping to sequester carbon from the atmosphere. So let's get in touch with our inner hunter-gatherer, have fun foraging and incorporate more sea vegetables into our diets.

A SHORT GUIDE TO EDIBLE SEAWEED

Dulse

Palmaria palmata
Dillisk or dulse is a favourite Irish seaweed, celebrated in both song and rhyme. This leafy red algae is usually eaten dried, its salty, mineral flavour often compared to bacon. Sprinkle a few flakes over your morning eggs.

Pepper dillisk

Osmundea pinnatifida
A true gastronomic treat, this tiny, brown, fern-like seaweed grows on rocks close to the shoreline and has a distinct flavour of truffles. Pick at low tide and nibble it raw, or add to broths, salads or crackers.

Corallina

Corallina officinalis
As its name suggests, this red-fronded seaweed looks
a little like floating coral. Tiny calcium deposits give
it a distinctive crunch. I particularly love it used raw
and combined with other seaweeds in salads with a
Japanese dressing.

Sea lettuce

Ulva lactuca
This easily identifiable seaweed looks like large leaves
of translucent green lettuce. My grandchildren love
to harvest it as it grows in rock pools close to the
shore. Tender and delicious added to salads or broths.

Carrageen moss

Chondrus crispus
The value of carrageen, which means 'little rock'
in Gaelic, has been passed from generation to
generation. Harvested from rocks exposed during
low tides, it was traditionally spread out to dry on
the spongy grass on the cliffs overlooking the sea,
washed by the rain and bleached by the sun for 8–10
days. The feather-light carrageen is a natural gelatine,
and can be used to thicken stews, and as a honey-
flavoured drink to soothe chesty coughs.

Ngapi
by MiMi Aye

There's an old saying that you can never be considered truly Burmese if you don't love *ngapi* – the joke goes that it runs through our veins, much like the Irrawaddy River flows through Burma.

Salty and packed with umami, ngapi is very similar to shrimp paste. Freshwater fish, small fry, sometimes shrimp or a combination of both, are trawled from the Irrawaddy, pounded to a paste with plenty of salt and then left to ferment in the baking sun. The word ngapi means 'pressed fish', or literally 'fish pressed', as our adjectives tend to follow the nouns.

I once came across an ancient edict by a bullish king of Thailand declaring that ngapi, which had become popular in his country, would henceforth be referred to as *kapi* in order to obscure its Burmese origins – a ridiculous decree reflecting the fact that we have never been good neighbours.

Ngapi is a great leveller in Burma, enjoyed throughout the year and across much of the land, regardless of class or background, although folk with rural accents are often teased for speaking with a ngapi twang.

As the main attraction, ngapi features in numerous Burmese dishes, all generally served with rice: fried into the tangy, sticky relish *ngapi kyaw* (or *balachaung*), which is enjoyed with practically everything, and is often slathered between slices of bread; cooked into a salty, savoury curry called *ngapi chet*; simmered into a spicy, piquant sauce known as *ngapi yay-kyo* into which crudités and blanched vegetables are dipped (much like *bagna cauda*); and – my favourite – pounded with lots of chillies and garlic into a fiery condiment known as *ngapi htaung*, which lifts any meal.

Think of ngapi as fish sauce with rocket boosters. We'll gladly toss it into any savoury dish in the same way that salt is used in the West and soy sauce in much of Asia.

This magic ingredient gives a particularly rousing kick to the Burmese dish *theezohn chinyay hin* (vegetable sour soup) – a lavish but soothing broth that's served as a side dish in Burma, but is just as wonderful as a starter, or even ladled over rice. The medley of vegetables also means it's a wonderful way to welcome the harvest, so in Britain it's a perfect September treat.

THEEZOHN CHINYAY HIN

Serves 4–6

2 onions, 1 sliced and 1 roughly chopped
1 spring onion
1 very ripe tomato, roughly chopped
2 tbsp tomato purée
1cm (½in) piece of fresh ginger, peeled
4 garlic cloves
4 tbsp groundnut oil
½ tsp ground turmeric
1 tbsp ngapi or shrimp paste
1 tsp garam masala or medium curry powder
1 tbsp dried shrimp
1 tbsp rice flour or cornflour

1 drumstick vegetable (*Moringa oleifera*), chopped into 5cm (2in) sections (optional)
1 large carrot, chopped into 2cm (¾in) chunks
3 eggs
6cm (2½in) piece of daikon (mooli), sliced, or 8 radishes, trimmed
8 okra pods, trimmed
10 green beans, trimmed
1 tbsp tamarind paste
100g (3½oz) spinach leaves
3 tbsp fish sauce
½ tsp sugar
½ tsp MSG

Put the chopped onion, spring onion, tomato, tomato purée, ginger and garlic in a blender and blitz to a smooth paste.

Heat the oil in a large saucepan over a high heat. Add the turmeric and sizzle for a few seconds. Reduce the heat to medium, then add the onion paste and fry for 10 minutes until fragrant. Add the ngapi, garam masala, dried shrimp and rice flour, and fry, stirring, for a further 3–4 minutes.

Pour in 1.5 litres (3½ pints) of water and add the drumstick, if using, and the carrot. Turn the heat back up to high and bring to a vigorous boil, then reduce to medium once more and simmer for 5 minutes. Add the eggs, sliced onion and the daikon, simmer for a further 10 minutes, then remove the hard-boiled eggs. Peel and halve the eggs, then return them to the pan with the okra, green beans, tamarind paste and spinach. Continue simmering for a further 10 minutes until the onion and daikon are soft and translucent, the spinach wilted, and carrots and green beans tender.

Stir in the fish sauce, sugar and MSG, and ladle the broth into bowls, making sure each one has a mix of vegetables and some egg.

An Autumn Appetite

by Diana Henry

New school shoes with toes as glossy as conkers; unfamiliar textbooks, the smell of them making you both excited and jittery; blackberry-picking along the empty roads near home, coming back with saucepans of fruit and stained T-shirts. This is September, the most unsettling month but also the one that is full of possibilities. Returning to school marks a new phase, a timetable that doesn't just cover the school day but the entire week, at home as well as in the classroom. Even though it's been years since my life was divided into school terms, I've never shaken off this feeling of September newness.

Early in the month, we cling to the last vestiges of summer and wonder every day what season it is. There are big blue-sky days whose light becomes milky in the late afternoon, and others that are flat, the colour of steel. The contrast between summer and autumn is extreme, but it takes a whole month to happen.

For the cook, September is a heady month, the abundance almost embarrassing, the collision of ingredients exhilarating. I make sweetcorn soup with wild mushrooms, mackerel with pickled damsons, melon and raspberries with a little herb syrup. At first, there's an overlap with late August, both in weather and in ingredients. Some September days call for sunshine cooking – I love the last barbecues, griddling chicken thighs that have been marinated with oregano, black pepper and chilli – the last hoorah of summer before we turn to stews. I want to make the most of the stone fruit too, but the way I cook it changes. Peach tart isn't right – too sweet, too pretty – but peaches baked with brown butter and maple syrup are. I fancy the syrup tastes of the leaves that are beginning to turn.

Aubergines, figs, plums and blackberries are the ingredients that most sum up September for me. It's no coincidence that they're all purple. The gaudy reds of summer are on their way out. Figs appear in August but carry all the softness of autumn, their inky skin sketched with pastels, smudged with a thumb and forefinger. Aubergine flesh has something of both summer and autumn about it – roasted, it collapses into softness; griddled, it tastes smoky, like the gauzy October days that are on their way.

Blackberries can be so drunk on summer sun they are hard to pick, their juice released as soon as you touch them. In warmer, southern parts, blackberries can be finished by the end of August. In Northern Ireland, where I'm from, and all points north, in fact, they're both a late summer and an autumn fruit. They can share a plate with poached nectarines or be tumbled into a big bowl for blackberry and apple crumble.

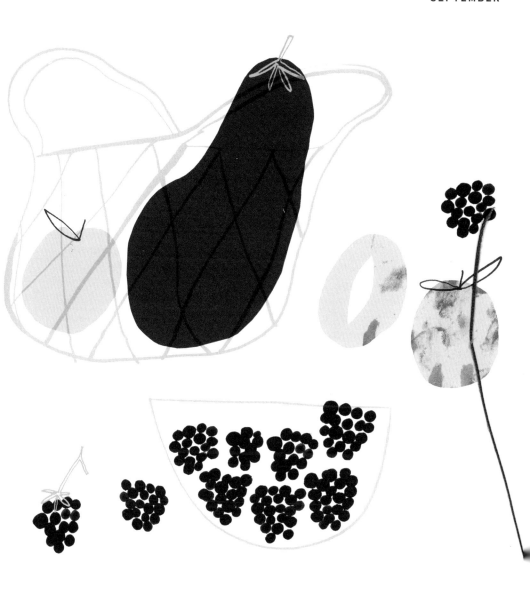

Once autumn has properly arrived, the first meal I invite friends to feels significant. It's my own small harvest festival. I happily greet the pumpkins and sleepy fat-bottomed pears, cobnuts in their ribbed coats and plump-cheeked apples. These ingredients are signifiers of order for me, quite unlike the foods that appeal to the fickle appetites of summer. By the end of the month, this is what I accept and give way to – a more defined schedule, more time in the kitchen, the comfort of order.

Bottled Sunshine

by Pam Corbin

There's an ambrosial sweetness about September, the peak of the preserving year. There's plenty to do, but what a joy it is to linger in the autumn sun, gathering in the summer's bounty, and then spend a few hours jamming, potting, pickling and transforming the abundance into something exciting to store away and feast upon later in the year.

Locality and climate play a big hand in when our magnificent orchard fruits are ready. Nonetheless, the beginning of September generally sees plenty of plums, apples and pears, ahead of the fragrant quince later in the month. For centuries, these treasures of our native orchards have been at the heart of so many store-cupboard preserves – jams, jellies, chutneys, pickles, old-fashioned bottled fruits – and with a welcome resurgence of home preserving alongside the growing awareness of the provenance of our foods, it is marvellous to see these traditional skills flourishing once more.

But the orchard does not provide for the preserver's pot alone. There are rich pickings everywhere in September. For foragers, the hedgerows are radiant with burnished reds, scarlets and the berry-black hues of characterful fruits; blackberries, crab apples, rowans, elderberries, rosehips, haws and the blue-bloomed sloes are there for the taking. Most are crammed with pips and pits and are best deployed as hedgerow jellies, health-boosting cordials and ketchups using methods that include straining or sieving the seed-filled fruits.

In the veg patch, there is a never-ending supply of long green beans, courgettes, marrows, pumpkins, cucumbers, caulis, pearly onions, ripening tomatoes and more. Less acidic than the orchard and hedgerow produce, vegetables lend themselves most favourably to the bright sharpness of vinegar and warming spices to preserve and flavour them.

September gives resplendently; a month to cherish. Let us waste not, nor want not – the responsibility is ours to take, and we should value the wholesomeness this glorious month hands to us so very generously.

PRESERVING TIPS FOR SEPTEMBER

Seeds

Nasturtium seeds are edible and have a spicy, peppery flavour. Add to piccalilli mixes, or lightly pickle and use as an alternative to capers. Gather the spherical seeds on a warm, dry day, selecting only the tender green ones (yellowing ones tend to be dry and strong in flavour). To pickle: cold brine in 300ml (10fl oz) water and 15g (½oz) salt for a few hours. Drain. Pack into a jar with a few peppercorns and cover with white wine vinegar.

Stems

Don't waste pruning trimmings from cutting back the mature stems of perennial herbs such as rosemary, lavender, lemon verbena and thyme – they are rich in essence and aroma. Add to poaching apples or damsons to produce a full-flavoured fruit stock for jelly-making.

Berries

Blackberries ripen quickly and the earliest ones are the fattest and the best. Don't delay – pick when you see them or they'll be gone when you return. Capture their mellow, homely character in jams, jellies, fruit leathers and compotes, or steep in gin or whisky. If time is short, pop them in the freezer to use later in the year.

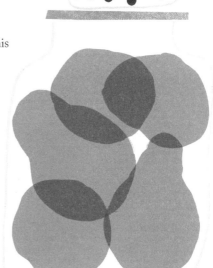

Orchard fruits

Don't overlook the pectin-rich quince. This hard fruit, with its irregular pear-like shape, canary-yellow peel and gorgeous fragrance is tricky to cut up when uncooked. For making quince cheese (*membrillo*), the easiest way to prepare quinces is to cook them whole in gently simmering water, then pull away the tender flesh from the woody core.

A Menu for September
by Emily Scott

ST AUSTELL BAY MUSSELS WITH FENNEL AND SAFFRON CREAM

Cooking with the ebb and flow of nature gives me so much joy. Autumn tides bring beautiful Cornish blue mussels, harvested sustainably in the local bays and estuaries. Grown on ropes in the nutrient-rich waters of the Gulf Stream that wraps around the West Country coastline, the mussels are particularly plump and sweet at this time of year.

Serves 2

```
1.5kg (3lb 5oz) fresh mussels, shells scrubbed then rinsed
2 tbsp olive oil
2 shallots, chopped
2 garlic cloves, finely chopped
1 fennel bulb and fronds, finely sliced
1 tbsp finely chopped flat-leaf parsley, plus extra to serve
250ml (9fl oz) white wine
250ml (9fl oz) double cream
2 pinches of saffron
1 tbsp lemon juice
Sea salt and freshly ground black pepper
```

Discard any mussels that do not close firmly after a good tap on a work surface and any with broken shells. Soak the rest in fresh water for 15 minutes to remove any sand, then pull off their beards with a sharp tug.

Place a large saucepan over a medium heat. Add the olive oil, shallots, garlic and fennel and cook, stirring, for 5 minutes or until softened. Add the parsley, wine, cream and saffron. Bring to the boil and then simmer gently for 5 minutes. The cream will turn a life-enhancing burnished yellow colour. Add the mussels and increase the heat to high. Cover with a tight-fitting lid and cook for 4–5 minutes, giving the saucepan an occasional shake. Uncover and stir well. Spoon the mussels into two serving bowls, discarding any that have not opened.

Reduce the sauce for 2 minutes, then add a squeeze of lemon and season to taste, before pouring over the mussels. Garnish with chopped parsley and serve immediately with crusty bread to mop up the delicious creamy sauce.

CORNISH FISH PIE WITH SOFT LEEKS AND CELERIAC MASH

I love fish pie, so comforting and hearty for the colder autumn evenings. This is a nod to Cornwall with a mixture of sustainably sourced white and smoked fish, sweet leeks and spinach in a creamy sauce, topped with the underrated autumnal hero: mashed celeriac, which adds a wonderful nuttiness and depth of flavour.

Serves 4

650g (1lb 7oz) fish pie mix, including white fish, salmon and
undyed smoked haddock
80g (2¾oz) unsalted butter
500ml (18fl oz) milk
1 bay leaf
4 black peppercorns
Grated nutmeg
40g (1½oz) plain flour
3 leeks, trimmed and thinly sliced
5 tbsp chopped flat-leaf parsley
200g (7oz) baby spinach
Sea salt and freshly ground black pepper

For the celeriac mash:
1 celeriac
3 potatoes
100g (3½oz) unsalted butter
50ml (2fl oz) double cream
50g Parmesan, grated

Peel the celeriac and potatoes and cut into roughly 2.5cm (1in) cubes. Place in a saucepan and cover with water. Bring to the boil and simmer for 15–20 minutes until a knife easily pierces them. Drain well and mash with half the butter (keep the rest for baking the pie) and all of the cream. Season to taste and set aside.

Preheat the oven to 180°C/350°F/gas mark 4.

Check the fish for any obvious bones, but keep the skin in place for the moment. Place all the fish in a large saucepan and pour over the milk, just to cover. Add the bay leaf, peppercorns and a grating of nutmeg. Place over a low heat, turning it down just before the milk boils. Turn off the heat and let the fish stand for 10 minutes, then carefully remove the fish and strain the milk into a jug. Remove the skin from the fish and discard. Set the skinned fish aside.

Melt half the butter in a pan over a medium heat. Add the leeks and allow to soften but not colour, then set aside while you make the sauce.

Melt the remaining butter in a small saucepan over a low heat. Stir in the flour and cook, stirring constantly, until it turns a pale biscuit colour. Pour in the reserved warm milk from cooking the fish, stirring with a whisk until smooth. It will thicken and turn beautifully glossy.

Carefully fold in the fish, then season and add the chopped parsley. Fold in the leeks, along with the spinach and transfer to an ovenproof dish. Cover the fish with the mash. Add a little extra sea salt, dot with knobs of butter and sprinkle with grated Parmesan. Bake for 20 minutes until golden brown and bubbling.

CHOCOLATE AND BLACKBERRY ROULADE

This rich chocolate roulade filled with blackberries and Chantilly cream is always a crowd-pleaser. For a bit of spectacle, bring it to the table on a large serving plate decorated with autumn foliage.

Serves 8

500g (1lb 2oz) dark chocolate
150ml (5fl oz) warm water
300g (10½oz) caster sugar
10 medium eggs, separated
500ml (18fl oz) double cream
25g (1oz) icing sugar
Seeds from 1 vanilla pod
350g (12oz) blackberries
Icing sugar, to decorate

Preheat the oven to 190°C/375°F/gas mark 5 and line a Swiss roll tin with baking paper.

Break the chocolate into small pieces and melt over a bain marie. Add the measured warm water to the melted chocolate and stir, then remove from the heat and set aside to cool slightly.

Meanwhile, whisk the sugar and egg yolks together until thick and fluffy. Add the cooled, melted chocolate to the mixture. Wash and dry the beaters, then put the egg whites into a large clean bowl and whisk until stiff. Carefully fold the egg whites into the chocolate mixture. Pour into the prepared tin and bake for 12–15 minutes. Remove from the oven and place a clean, damp tea towel over the sponge – this will create steam as it cools, which helps make the sponge easier to roll. Allow to cool.

For the Chantilly, whip the cream with the icing sugar and vanilla seeds until thick enough to spread, but be careful not to take it so far that it curdles.

Remove the damp tea towel from the sponge and turn out onto a fresh sheet of baking paper. Spread the whipped cream over the surface, leaving a gap at both ends. Cover with blackberries and dust with icing sugar. Using the baking paper to help you, roll up the roulade like a Swiss roll. Do not worry if it cracks; this adds character. Place on a wooden board and dust with more icing sugar – a great way to hide any imperfections, although I am rather fond of them. Eat with happiness and extra cream if feeling indulgent.

Reading List

Darina Allen,
Forgotten Skills of Cooking
A modern guide to traditional cookery skills, covering everything from keeping chickens to foraging to making your own butter, sourdough and cider.

Miek Zwamborn,
Seaweed
An exquisitely illustrated miscellany of seaweed by the Dutch poet and artist, sharing her discoveries of its history, culture and use, from the Neolithic people of the Orkney Islands to sushi masters in modern Japan.

MiMi Aye,
Mandalay
A love letter to Burmese food, with personal stories, family photos and recipes for fritters, noodles, salads and sweet snacks. Try the Burmese tofu fritters and sticky rice doughnuts.

Diana Henry,
From the Oven to the Table
Simple dishes that look after themselves, for when the weather turns and the warmth of the oven is welcome: baked sausages with apples and blackberries; autumn vegetables with walnut-miso sauce; ginger-roast plums with muscovado cream.

Pam Corbin,
Pam the Jam
Perfect preserves from the expert every professional cook consults, with recipes for all the classic jams, jellies, marmalades, chutneys and pickles, as well as more unusual ideas, such as lime and coconut curd.

Emily Scott,
Sea and Shore
Seasonal recipes that follow the ebb and flow of the rugged Cornish coastline. Flick to the useful interludes on Port Isaac, pasties and wild swimming if you're planning a visit.

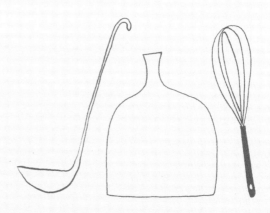

October

October is the apple of many a cook's eye. Fresh produce abounds, the days draw in and the warm glow of the kitchen tempts once more. The heft of squashes and pumpkins adds weight to hearty dishes, and delicate wild mushrooms provide a touch of luxury, fried in butter and served on toast. Rustling walks through fiery foliage, cider brandy hot toddies sipped in the cool, crisp air, and sturdy English puddings, transformed by steam, made from recipes that have remained the same for generations.

IN SEASON

Apples
Autumn truffles
Borlotti beans
Cardoons
Grapes
Juniper berries
Pears

Pumpkins
Quince
Romanesco
Rosehips
Squash
Sweet chestnuts
Wild mushrooms

Apples

After the summer flush of crisp, early apples, comes the windfall of the orchard's harvest. The season for this hardy British fruit is impressively long – from the first Discovery in August to the last Cornish Gilliflower coming out of store as winter wanes. There is poetry in their names and delight to be found in the thousands of varieties growing on our shores. Seek out heritage varieties, such as Veitch's Perfection, with its sharp bite and lingering nuttiness – a characteristic the Victorians and Edwardians sought for pairing apple desserts with port – or Old Somerset Russet, with its refreshing pineapple tang.

One of the first fruits to have been cultivated, the apple as we know it is very different from its wild ancestors (though tiny, sour crab apples still make a delectable jelly). Some of our most beloved apple dishes are of medieval origin; culinary texts of the fourteenth century give recipes for apple sauce, fritters, pies and tarts, as well as a curious apple soup made with beef broth or almond milk.

Dividing apples into cooking and eating varieties is a very British distinction – a somewhat confusing affectation for which we can thank the Victorians – but it is worth considering the best apple for the job. Nigel Slater splits apples into two kinds: 'those that will look good in soldierly slices under the glaze of a fruit tart, and those that will melt into a sweet, fragrant slush'. Choose frothing apples such as Bramley or Grenadier for baking, Blenheim Orange for an open tart, and aromatic apples such as Ashmead's Kernel for eating with a wedge of cheese. To test whether your chosen apple will hold its shape under heat, simply cook a slice in the oven or in a pan and watch to see if it bursts into a cloud-like froth.

Apples shine in British puddings, from crumble to apple charlotte, yet this versatile fruit is just as happy paired with roast pork or game, sliced raw with fennel or chicory in slaws and salads, or chopped into chutneys. Cut a crisp apple with a stubby fruit knife and pair with a farmhouse cheese for an impromptu autumn snack, or heat the grill and hide thinly sliced fried apples under a blanket of cheese for a twist on Welsh rarebit.

We may have lost many of our varieties to the homogeneity of the supermarket shelves, but our rich apple heritage lives on in wassailing and Halloween apple-bobbing. Seek out your local Apple Day this month and celebrate the harvest with a glass of cider and a renewed appreciation for the fruit of paradise.

Cider Brandy
by James Rich

As autumn begins to show its colours and the silent, drifting leaves form crisp layers that crunch pleasingly underfoot, it's a time to reflect and recharge. For me, this is the season of slow, meandering walks through the orchards of my home county of Somerset, famous for its acres of apple trees and its cider.

At any time of year, these old orchards are a place of wonder: the gnarly apple trees, resplendent with fragrant blossom in spring, and lush, green canopy to laze beneath in summer, yield their bountiful crop of fruit come autumn. Even in winter, stripped bare of foliage and fruit, the trees create a somewhat eerie wilderness, especially in the cold mists of morning.

For millennia, orchards have been a source of nourishment, from the fresh fruit and hedgerow forage to the pressed juice and ferments. Yet cider brandy is still a little-known orchard treat. Distilled from cider into *eau de vie* – 'water of life' – and matured in oak casks for as many as 20 years, Somerset cider brandy is a robust yet mellow spirit equal in body and flavour to its more famous French sibling, Calvados.

Cider brandy has a tantalisingly evocative effect, transporting you back to its origin. Take a sip, close your eyes and savour those heady autumnal aromas: the crisp, cold closeness of the orchard air filled with herbaceous and fruity scent. It's all there, captured in every single drop.

SOMERSET CIDER BRANDY HOT TODDY

Makes 1

50ml (2fl oz) Somerset cider brandy
1 tbsp runny honey
1 cinnamon stick
1 dried apple slice (use fresh if you don't have any dried)
1 lemon slice

Boil the kettle. Add the cider brandy, honey and cinnamon stick to a mug or heatproof glass. Top up with just-boiled water and stir to dissolve the honey. Add the apple and lemon slice and enjoy next to a roaring fire.

Three Particular Puddings
by Simon Hopkinson

The very finest of English puddings are, it seems, often made using the plainest ingredients: beef suet, leftover bread, a couple of eggs, a lemon or two, a spoonful of jam, a touch of spice and always, but always, a healthy pinch of salt. Here are three favourites:

SUSSEX POND PUDDING

Quite simply, a rich suet crust, a whole lemon, butter and brown sugar, steamed in a basin for a good three hours and turned out onto a deep dish. The expectation is that, once cut, a pool – 'the pond' – of lemon-scented butterscotch sauce will emerge from within. Well, this does not always happen, but it matters not; some misguided modern cooks have attempted to exaggerate the pond by pouring in a pre-made liquid of the butter and sugar mixture at the start, which is folly. Even if the pudding is not a looker, its flavour is sublime – and what many now seem to forget is that the pudding is all about the suet crust! Roughly 140g (5oz) suet to 200g (7oz) self-raising flour works well, with a handful of soft white breadcrumbs to lighten it and a little extra baking powder. The pastry should be rolled quite thick, so that it absorbs most of the lemon-fragrant butter and sugar. One may only have a 'puddle', but it's the sogged suet crust that counts.

QUEEN OF PUDDINGS

My mother made queen of puddings regularly and it was adored by all. Eggs, jam, milk and breadcrumbs have never been so magically transformed before or since. I'm not one to meddle much with tradition, but I have used brioche crumbs for some time now, and occasionally, in summer, I will stew a punnet of raspberries to replace the so-sweet jam. Otherwise, the song remains the same. A final, light dusting of caster sugar over the meringue (learnt from mother) before it goes into the oven – and it *must* go into the oven – will produce the most wonderful, essential crust. And that final bake must actually *cook* the meringue; I usually allow a good 15–20 minutes at about 150°C/300°F/gas mark 2, which produces a gorgeous, pale golden finish. A silly blowtorch achieves nothing more than a sad, leathery blister and raw meringue beneath. Lecture complete.

BAKEWELL PUDDING

A part of my school education took place in Derbyshire and home was Lancashire. Conveniently, and deliciously, the route home at the end of term passed close by the town of Bakewell, where its eponymous pudding (most definitely never a tart!) originated. Sara Paston-Williams, in her excellent *National Trust Book of Traditional Puddings*, goes into much detail about the origins of the pudding, as well as giving a recipe that, unless you have been to The Old Original Bakewell Pudding Shop and eaten one, produces such a unique marvel of confectionery that it will astonish those who, hitherto, have known only Mr Kipling. Traditionally, there would be chopped candied peel as well as jam at the base of the pudding. Unusually, the butter in the filling (essentially a frangipane) is melted; while flavourings, such as vanilla or ratafia (now, more commonly, almond essence) and brandy (I prefer rum) further enhance. The melted butter creates a filling that emerges almost custard-like, just set and utterly delectable. I have never used the suggested bits of candied peel, simply because they interrupt the texture of the soft filling, almost as interlopers. Just jam, for me. Raspberry is traditional, but try apricot, too.

Silken Egg Custard
by Zing Tsjeng

Steam was one of the many things that baffled me when I first came to the UK. Not steam trains or engines, but the act of steaming, which British people apply judiciously to vegetables to throttle them to a limp, soggy death. Worn-out runner beans that resembled a corpse's limp fingers; broccoli florets leached of colour and substance – this was considered a healthy and optimal way of cooking food. Even now, you'll see these sad-looking greens pop up in fitness influencers' Instagram posts, next to an overcooked, meaty fist of chicken breast.

Back home in Singapore, steaming is a delicate art – as it is in several Asian countries, including Japan, Korea and China. Steam helps bring out the precise flavours of food with little to no seasoning required – you could steam a chicken with nothing but ginger and spring onions, and it would taste as chicken-y as the day it strolled out of the hen coop.

Nowhere is this more evident than with eggs, which Asian cooks mix with water, dashi, chicken stock or milk and steam in bowls to serve as either a savoury dish or a sweet treat. The hot vapour gently warms and cooks the beaten eggs into a silky, tofu-like curd that is deceptively light and utterly delicious. It's sometimes called steamed egg custard, although purists will insist that the 'custard' is superfluous.

My first memory of eating steamed egg is as a child at the Goodwood Park Hotel in Singapore; it gently slipped down my throat with the kind of warming quality you associate with only your mum's food. Given its simplicity, some of the best steamed egg you'll find is usually cooked by mothers, my own included – though she had to have a few potholed goes before nailing *chawanmushi*, the Japanese equivalent, which is served in teacups, dotted with gingko nuts, shiitake mushrooms and other tiny garnishes.

The recipe below is the Chinese version, as cooked by my mother for our family dinners. You can find salted raw duck eggs and century or preserved eggs at most Asian supermarkets, but you can also omit either or both of them – just add half a teaspoon of salt into the egg mixture to compensate, or ramp up the amount of soy sauce. You're aiming for the surface of the steamed egg to be as smooth and flat as a pool of still water, though you can easily disguise any unsightly pockmarks with soy sauce or garnishes. Serve with white rice.

STEAMED EGG

Serves 4 as a side, or 2 as a main

4 fresh eggs, at room temperature
2 salted raw duck eggs, with the liquid egg whites and soft
yolks separated and the latter finely chopped
2 century eggs, finely chopped
1 tbsp neutral vegetable oil
1 spring onion, finely chopped, to garnish

Use chopsticks to gently whisk the fresh eggs with the egg white of the salted duck eggs.

Measure the volume of the egg mixture and add 1½ times that amount of water. Gently whisk again with chopsticks and sieve the liquid into a bowl or deep plate, scooping away any foam or bubbles on the surface. Scatter the chopped egg yolks and century eggs into the liquid mixture.

Tightly cover the bowl with foil and place on a steamer plate set in a wok or shallow saucepan. Pour boiling water into the wok or pan, ensuring the bowl itself is not in contact with the water. Put the lid on and steam the mixture over a low heat for 20–30 minutes, or until the egg is set.

Warm the oil in a small pan, pour it over the egg and drizzle with the soy sauce. Serve garnished with the spring onion.

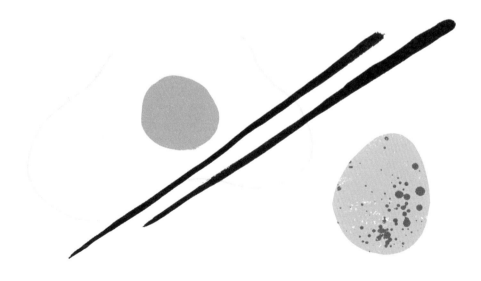

A Menu for October

by Jeremy Lee

SALT MALLARD AND PICKLED PRUNES

One mallard will feed two or three modest trenchermen. Bear in mind that this dish will require 48 hours to complete: not the cooking, just salting the bird beforehand. Make lots of pickled prunes as they cook better en masse and keep very well, jollying along all manner of cold meats, terrines and suchlike.

Serves 2–3

1 mallard
1 bay leaf
1 thyme sprig
Sea salt and freshly ground black pepper

For the prunes:
250g (9oz) redcurrant jelly
150ml (5fl oz) red wine vinegar
500g (1lb 2oz) unpitted prunes
½ cinnamon stick
1 tsp black peppercorns, ground
1 bay leaf
2 strips of lemon zest
2 strips of orange zest
Watercress, to serve

To prepare the mallard, cut away the backbone, then the wishbone. Exert pressure to flatten the bird slightly before laying in a small crock or a similar vessel.

Strew the mallard with a teaspoon of sea salt, then the result of six turns of the pepper mill. Pop in the bay leaf and the thyme. Cover it well and place in the fridge to marinate overnight or preferably for 24 hours.

To cook the mallard, bring a large pan of water to the boil. Lift the bird from the crock and slip it into the water. Return the water to a simmer and let the bird cook for 10–15minutes depending on its size.

Using a pair of sturdy tongs, carefully transfer the mallard to a small tray and leave to cool.

Meanwhile, prepare the prunes. Put the jelly and vinegar in a wide-based pan over a gentle heat. Add the prunes, cinnamon stick, ground pepper, bay leaf and strips of citrus rind. Simmer together for 5 minutes, stirring gently, then remove from the heat. Keep a few aside for your mallard and transfer the rest to a clean container with a close-fitting lid. Seal and then store in a cool spot.

When ready to serve, remove the duck legs and cut in half. Remove the breasts and slice thinly. Heap all the meat onto a serving platter alongside a small bunch of watercress. Serve with the pickled prunes.

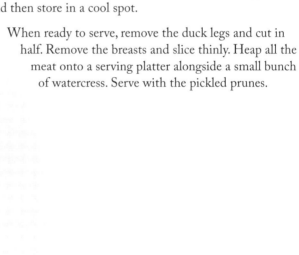

GRILLED MACKEREL WITH GREEN TOMATO AND DILL SALAD

The salty crust that forms on the silver skin of a mackerel as it grills belies the delicacy of the fish once cooked. A good foil for this sublime oily fish is a salad with real bite, spiked with mustard. A felicitous, not to mention favourite, pairing on the plate. This salad is also the perfect way for veg growers to use any green tomatoes that have not ripened in the fading heat of autumn. Look out for Tropea onions, an Italian variety that is far sweeter than your average red onion.

Serves 4

4 mackerel, of a size pleasing enough to keep whole
1 cucumber, peeled and halved lengthways
Pinch of sugar
A splash of apple cider vinegar
1 tsp Dijon mustard
5 tbsp extra virgin olive oil
1 tbsp chopped dill fronds
4 green tomatoes, diced
2 small apples, peeled, cored and diced
2 Tropea or red onions, thinly sliced
Sea salt and freshly ground black pepper
2 lemons, halved, to serve

Slit open the belly of each mackerel and remove the guts. Clean the insides of any residual blood, then pat the fish dry.

Using a teaspoon, remove the seeds from the cucumber halves. Cut the halves into slices, slightly angled and about 8–10mm (⅜-½in) thick. Tip into a bowl and toss with a teaspoon of salt. Leave to sit for an hour or so. Wash thoroughly under cold running water, then drain.

Whisk a pinch of sugar, salt and pepper with the vinegar in a large bowl. Add the mustard and mix well. Add the oil, a spoonful at a time, whisking all the while. Those of a bolder nature might wish to add more mustard for punch; I generally always do. Stir in the chopped dill.

Squeeze the cucumber dry in a clean tea towel. Tip into the bowl with the dressing, along with the prepared tomatoes, apples and onions. Mix well.

Place a griddle pan over a medium heat and when hot, though not infernal, strew with sea salt and lay the fish thereon. Leave the fish to cook undisturbed: strengthen your resolve and do not be tempted to lift the fish to peek. If you do, it will lessen the crust and, heaven forbid, encourage the fish to stick. Courage is necessary here, as well as 7 or 8 minutes, by which time the edges of the mackerel

will have taken on an appealing dark hue. Lift and turn with care, revealing a splendid crust. Continue to cook for a further 5 minutes or so. Gently lifting the incision to the belly will reveal how the fish is cooking along the backbone. It is worth noting here that minimum cooking makes for far better eating.

Place the cooked mackerel on plates and serve with lemon halves for squeezing and the salad heaped alongside. This dish is delicious eaten warm or cold.

FRANGIPANE TART WITH CARAMELISED APPLES

Marcona almonds are softer and sweeter than the usual variety and they make the best frangipane. There is no point making this tart on a smaller scale. Enjoy the leftovers with glee over the coming days, served with a tub of the naughtiest, thickest Jersey cream.

Serves 12

For the pastry:
250g (9oz) plain flour, plus extra for dusting
125g (4½oz) unsalted butter, cold, plus extra for greasing
Pinch of sea salt
50g (1¾oz) icing sugar
2 egg yolks
1 tsp cold water

```
For the frangipane:
500g (1lb 2oz) Marcona almonds
500g (1lb 2oz) unsalted butter, softened
500g (1lb 2oz) caster sugar
4 eggs

For the apples:
6 apples (Jonagold, Discovery or Cox are good for this)
100g (3½oz) caster sugar
2 lemons

Thick Jersey cream, to serve
```

To make the pastry, put the flour, butter, salt and icing sugar in a food processor. Pulse to render everything to a fine crumb. Add the egg yolks and water. Whizz until a ball begins to form. Tip onto a board and knead lightly and quickly. Wrap well and keep in the fridge for at least 1 hour, preferably overnight.

To make the frangipane, grind the almonds in a food processor to a coarse crumb. Beat the butter with the sugar until just mixed. Add the eggs, one at a time, then stir in the almonds. Transfer to a container, cover and refrigerate until ready to bake.

Preheat the oven to 160°C/325°F/gas mark 3. Position a shelf in the middle of the oven and place a baking tray below it on a second shelf. Grease and flour a 28cm (11in) fluted tart tin with sides 3cm (1¼in) deep.

Remove the pastry from the fridge and roll out on a lightly floured surface until about 2–3mm (⅛in) thick. Line the tart tin with the pastry, trimming off the excess. Add the frangipane until four-fifths full. Bake in the oven for 1 hour, then reduce the temperature to 130°C/260°F/gas mark ¾ for a further 15 minutes. Remove from the oven and leave to cool.

Meanwhile, peel, core and slice the apples into sixths. Put the sugar in a heavy-based saucepan over a medium heat and dissolve, stirring, into a caramel. Add the apples and lemon juice carefully – the juice will cause the boiling sugar to splutter. Cook the apples boldly to ensure a good colour, banishing too much sweetness. Remove from the heat and leave to cool.

Unmould the tart onto a board, leave the apples in the pan and take them, along with the very naughty cream, to the table.

Reading List

Angela King and Sue Clifford,
The Apple Source Book
A charming and considered book to
dip into throughout the apple season,
with useful information on varieties,
orchards and wildlife, as well as recipes
from chefs and food writers including
Raymond Blanc, Fergus Henderson
and Delia Smith.

James Rich,
Apple: Recipes from the Orchard
Recipes for all the wonderful
ingredients to be found in hedgerows,
orchards and kitchen gardens, set
against the idyllic backdrop of the
author's countryside home in Somerset.

Simon Hopkinson,
Roast Chicken and Other Stories
A rich and comforting culinary
narrative from a classically trained
chef with the heart of a home cook.
A cookbook that belongs in every
kitchen and on every bedside table.

Harry Astley and Jane Scotter,
Fern Verrow
A fascinating account of farming life
with seasonal recipes and practical
advice, accompanied by stunning
photography by Tessa Traeger.

Sara Paston-Williams,
*The National Trust Book of
Traditional Puddings*
A collection of traditional recipes that
traces the history of British puddings
from the earliest medieval spiced
jellies through the elaborate pies of
the Elizabethans and Stuarts and the
elegant syllabubs and custards of the
Georgians, to the substantial puddings
of the Victorians.

Zing Tsjeng,
Forgotten Women: The Leaders
A compendium of remarkable women
campaigners, queens, politicians and
trailblazers, illustrated by a team of
female artists from all over the world.

Jeremy Lee,
Cooking
The simple joys of preparing and
cooking beautiful ingredients,
with recipes from the chef's home,
restaurant, family and friends, all told
with his signature wit and lyricism.

November

Time to slow down and recalibrate; let the morning mists clear. Root vegetables, long forgotten beneath the ground, take the limelight, as soothing and comforting as they are versatile. Discover the pleasures of unfamiliar fruits – medlars, sloes and the intoxicating scent of bergamots. As November draws to a close and autumn turns to winter, prepare for the festivities ahead with a flurry of kitchen activity and a generous dram of spiced rum.

IN SEASON

Bergamot
Cauliflower
Cavolo nero
Celeriac
Chervil root
Cranberries

Horseradish
Kohlrabi
Medlars
Parsley root
Salsify
Sloes

Celeriac

KNOBBLY GNARLY KNOTS

The knotted tendrils of celeriac hold fast to the ground it's pulled from, challenging you to unearth its inner beauty. There is pearly flesh beneath its monstrous exterior, and compelling culinary possibilities. When raw, its mineral notes and earthy quality are best captured with the bite of vinegar or lemon juice, yet its flavour mellows when cooked, softening to a subtle nuttiness with just a hint of underlying sweetness – a characteristic brought to the fore when caramelised in a hot oven.

Look for small, heavy roots, preferably with the fresh green shoots attached. A peeler won't mark the tough, gnarly skin – better to carve it away with a sharp knife. The white flesh browns quickly when exposed to air, so plunge pieces into lemon or vinegar-spiked water as you chop.

As the name suggests, celeriac is a kind of celery, cultivated for its bulbous root rather than its long stalks and serrated leaves. And, like celery, it contains a compound called phthalide that accentuates the flavours of other ingredients. Perhaps this is why it can sway from delicate to robust, never overpowering a dish, yet assertive enough to take on the heat of horseradish, chilli or garlic without losing its identity.

Celeriac enjoys the company of other winter roots and can happily impersonate a potato with its creamy colour and its ability to be boiled, roasted or mashed. Its versatility is partly due to its changing texture; firm when raw, yet yielding to a rich, velvety purée when cooked. It's a marvel that a vegetable so apparently brutish can be so completely transformed.

FORGOTTEN ROOTS

Slender roots, such as chervil, parsley and salsify, seem to have slipped from our culinary map. Parsley root, also known as Hamburg parsley, is a large-rooted variety of the familiar herb. Though it has all but disappeared from our own tables, you'll still find it in kitchens across Germany and Eastern Europe (it's an essential element in authentic borscht). Like celeriac, it can be eaten raw, roasted, boiled for mash or made into chips. Mark Diacono suggests shallow-frying thin strips of parsley root to make crisps, dusted with either salt and black pepper or sugar and cinnamon.

WHAT TO DO WITH CELERIAC

- Keep the trimmings for stock and use the slightly bitter leaves in place of celery or lovage in soups and stews.
- Forgo the prep and bake it whole, wrapped in foil with oil and herbs.
- Enjoy it raw – julienned into a remoulade or winter slaw with fennel and apple, or pair thin slices with blood orange and radicchio.
- Try Meera Sodha's hasselback celeriac, cutting deep fans into the root and smothering it in miso and tahini.
- Shave into thin ribbons to create a sort of 'pasta' – mimic maltagliati (Italian for 'badly cut') to make a feature of any irregularity – and serve with sage butter or slow-cooked ragu.
- Simmer into a silky soup and garnish with chestnuts or blue cheese.
- Pair with potatoes in a gratin, rösti or buttery mash and serve with sausages, game or a rich beef stew.
- Tempt out its sweet side – follow River Cottage's lead and churn into an eccentric ice cream.

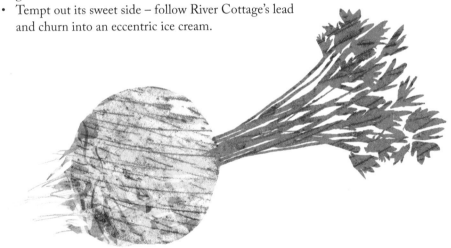

MAKE AHEAD

Horseradish vinegar

Fresh horseradish sauce will knock the socks off the jars you can buy in shops – but the flavour quickly wanes, so capture the root's fiery heat in vinegar to keep it raging on. Peel and grate fresh horseradish root and pack into a sterilised jar with shallots and a little sugar and salt. Cover with vinegar and leave for a month or so before straining and bottling. Perfect for pickling cucumber or beetroot, or to add a kick to salad dressings.

Yams

by Yemisi Aribisala

A yam tuber on a street stall in Golders Green reminds me of one of those Nigerian dignitaries at Heathrow – without paraphernalia of adoring entourage, no glaze bequeathed by beautiful heat and humidity – you know what I mean, diminished, affronted and prickly. Just waiting for someone to say the wrong word, to retort angrily, 'Don't you know who I am!'

For three years, I bought yams enthusiastically wherever I found them in London: on that stall in Golders Green, so beneath eye level that they might as well be invisible; at the supermarket, where I weighed them self-consciously, knowing the people waiting for the scales were curious about what I was buying, but too stiff upper lip to ask; from a Ghanaian woman who delivered them in cardboard boxes individually wrapped in beige sheets of paper.

My yams in Calabar were a strong contrast in their irrepressibility. You sometimes walked in on them conversing in the kitchen in the dark. They were not smooth-bodied, easily classified homogenous fellows that agreed to lie down in boxes. Wherever you placed them, they quickly pushed out amethyst purple fists, and in the following days, white fingers. You had to be vigilant in cutting away shoots on first sighting to keep the tuber fresh.

The very first time in my life I met the phenomenon called an Ogoja yam, it came by freight on Aero Contractors from Calabar to Lagos. It was at least the height of a toddler and the weight of two; an ugly, hairy, belligerent thing with nodules on every nodule. This is the real personality of the West African yam – more than food to the Nigerian. We grow over 70 per cent of all the yams eaten globally. Yams are a cultural symbol and come closest to that food which can be defined as 'our staff of life'. I always marvel at how we doggedly eat it throughout the year; through bitterness (new yams) to insect-ravaged woodiness (yams on their last legs).

My thoughts turn to how market women in the east of Nigeria – in Enugu, Onitsha, Ariaria – turn up their noses and declare the price of the yam (take it or leave it); how 40 yams from the bridegroom to the bride represent an undefined portion of the bride's ceremonial value or *trousseau*; how grown men grin and talk about their sexuality in the language of the yam; how Igbos and Ghanaians alike have an exuberant festival spiritually elevating the harvesting of new yams; how, with precise finickiness, we categorise yams for pounding, boiling, making pottage, for mucilaginous fritters (*ojojo*); how, by some magic, the yam becomes that other grey fluffy mound called *amala*; and how it elegantly gives body to soups like *afia efere* (white soup). The yam is unequivocally ours and we are fearless in its presence, no matter how belligerently it presents itself.

My relationship with yams is not so precious. I love yams cooked in pottage with ripe plantains. We call it yam porridge in Nigeria. Yes, by strict definition, porridge is grains or legumes boiled in water or milk or both. It must just be conceded that we have our own rationale for making the English language do what we want.

My recipe is also simple. The yam is cut into thick, round slices, the skin peeled off and discarded. Thereafter the yam slices are further cut into medium chunks, rinsed thoroughly and cooked briskly in salted boiling water. (A note to the uninitiated: if you handle cut yams and the uncooked saponins in the juice come into contact with your arms or face, they can set off an itch.)

The yam pieces are cooked when a fork goes through with some remaining resistance, breaking the pieces into smaller chunks, not mush. The yam is drained, the water kept to one side. Some pieces are mashed with a fork, to thicken the pottage nicely, and some are left whole. In a clean pan, shredded cabbage is briefly sautéed in coconut oil with aniseeds and half a habanero. A quarter of a tin of coconut milk is added to the sautéed cabbage, along with a bay leaf and seasonings, and the heat turned down to a simmer. Plantains cut into rounds are added and left to soften in the milk. The mashed and whole pieces of yam are then added, along with some of the reserved water, then stirred carefully until everything is well coated, trying not to break up the boiled pieces of yam. The heat is turned down low and the medley left until the gorgeous balance of sweet, savoury, bubbling hot and sticking-to-the-bottom-of-the-pan is achieved. The pottage can be finished with a handful of chopped kale, spread on its face and closed in with a lid, heat turned off.

Namkeen and Mithai
by Mallika Basu

Spheres of fresh paneer being lowered into bubbling sugar syrup. Battered and parcelled vegetables sizzling in oil until golden crisp. The aroma of saffron and green cardamom floating through the air. It must be Diwali.

Diwali celebrates the victory of good over evil, light over darkness and hope over despair across several communities and religions in India. Synonymous with terracotta *diyas* (lamps) and firecrackers, resplendent silks and bejewelled accessories, it is also a time of much divine and blessed sugar and ghee consumption.

Main meals enjoyed during Diwali are predominantly vegetarian. But this is when savoury snacks (*namkeen*) and sweet treats (*mithai*) come into their own – typically to be enjoyed with visitors at home and distributed among friends and family. Hand-decorated wooden crates and wicker platters, covered in tinted cellophane and gaudy ribbons would arrive at my metropolitan Calcutta home, filled to bursting with *samosas, laddoo, burfi* and *kachori*.

Mithai and namkeen are typically made by a seasoned expert *Halwai*, a snack maker, either in a shop or by special appointment at home. It takes true talent and time to manoeuvre vast vats of bubbling sugar and oil for large groups, and everyone I knew preferred to spend their time being fabulous.

Saying that, recreating traditional treats as homely projects is one of the many ways in which the Diwali-celebrating diaspora reconnects to the motherland at this auspicious time. Often featuring adjustments, adaptations and shortcuts, it's how we share the joys of the festive season with the ones we love. In my own home in London, we assemble milk powder burfi (similar to fudge) with more widely available cans of condensed milk, and we oven-bake samosas with ready-made shortcrust pastry and a sweet potato filling. It keeps my two children enthralled, despite the inevitable sugar crash.

Of course, it would be rude not to wash it all down with properly brewed masala chai. The best kind involves bubbling water and milk until it thickens slightly, and then adding aromatics like ginger and green cardamom and tea leaves. You can invite cloves, black pepper, saffron and more to the party, sugar is not an optional extra. In the true spirit of the season, dust off your festive finery, invite your friends round and, in the case of the diaspora, enjoy a taste of home away from home.

ADRAK MASALA CHAI

by Asma Khan

Serves 2

250ml (9fl oz) whole milk
5mm (¼in) piece fresh ginger, cut into small pieces
50g (1¾oz) soft light brown sugar
2.5cm (1in) long piece of cassia bark
6 green cardamom pods
6 cloves
2 tbsp loose-leaf strong black tea (such as Kenyan or Assam Orthodox), or any strong black teabag

Pour the milk and 1.5 litres (2¾ pints) water into a large saucepan and bring to the boil over a high heat. Add the ginger, sugar and all the spices. Reduce the heat to a low boil then leave, uncovered, for 20 minutes.

Add the loose-leaf tea and increase the heat until the liquid is boiling vigorously. After 1 minute, reduce the heat and allow the tea to simmer for 2 minutes. Increase the heat to high and boil the tea on full for a final minute.

Remove the pan from the heat, then strain the tea and serve hot.

A Kitchen in November
by Nina Mingya Powles

```
Ingredients:
a bowl of pears on the counter
a red persimmon sun
a collection of eggcups
a fox watching from her dark garden
a bitter moon

*

Scoop the yolk from a soft-boiled egg.
Crush salt crystals between your fingers.
Stock up on necessities: noodles, ginger, kimchi fizzing in
the fridge.
Rinse jasmine rice three times — swirl clockwise underwater.
Pay attention to the sky at moonrise.
Slowly and with care, gather the faraway parts of yourself.
Hold them gently (they contain hemispheres).
Buy cold clementines from the corner shop.
Peel them in a spiral motion, leaving the coiled skin unbroken,
the way your mother does.
```

Stir-up Sunday

PREPARING FOR CHRISTMAS

The last Sunday before Advent is traditionally the time to stir up your Christmas pudding. But there are lots of fun kitchen projects to embark on before the whirlwind of festive parties begins. Here are a few ideas to throw into the mix.

Drinks

Sloe gin will always be a welcome winter treat, but for some extra Christmas spirit, add warming spices such as cardamom, clove and star anise to a bottle of rum and let it slowly ruminate. Simple syrups can be simmered with seasonal fruits and spices too – a more versatile way to mix drinks whether you opt for virgin or boozy. Cranberries give a festive pop of red, or zest some bergamots for a fragrant champagne cocktail.

Treats

In Germany and across Scandinavia, Christmas preparations begin early, with families and friends gathering together to bake *lebkuchen* biscuits, marzipan-filled stollen and cinnamon stars. Follow their lead and fill the house with sugar and spice – the sturdiest biscuits can even be hung on the tree. Italian *biscotti* and *amaretti* also keep incredibly well – perfect for coffee breaks between Christmas shopping and present wrapping, or to share with impromptu guests.

Preserves

Prepare jars and bottles of flavourful preserves for all the generous cheeseboards you'll enjoy in December. Make spiced chutneys or a simple celery pickle – the most underrated of pickled veg. Homemade fruit jellies glowing next to snow-white cheeses always look festive, too. Try medlar, quince or a jelly made from Bramleys and whatever red or purple fruits you can get your hands on. For something really special, preserve whole, peeled pears in sugar, vinegar, herbs and spices to serve with ham, Stilton, terrines, and even Christmas pudding.

Gifts

Edible gifts are a joy to receive, full of thoughtfulness and warm wishes. Make crisp cheese toasts packed with dried fruit; spiced nuts; crystallised ginger; salted lemons and limes; marinated mushrooms glossed in olive oil; or perhaps Jane Grigson's clementines in armagnac. Candied orange peel takes time to make, but dipped in dark chocolate it's just right for when you want something small and sweet after a Christmas feast.

A Menu for November
by Helen Graves

CELERIAC AND MISO SOUP WITH POTATO AND ONION BREADSTICKS

This menu was written with a Bonfire Night gathering in mind, and this silky root vegetable soup can be handed out in mugs, with the soft potato and onion breadsticks a perfect shape for dunking. I think soup always needs a finishing touch, and here it's a swirl of miso butter and a sprinkle of *pul biber* – the gentle heat and sun-soaked chilli flavour is very welcome in November.

Serves 10

For the soup:
220g (8oz) unsalted butter
1 onion, diced
1 celery stick, sliced
150ml (5fl oz) white wine
1 celeriac (around 1.2kg/2lb 10oz), peeled and trimmed (prepared weight 900g/2lb)
2 bay leaves
1 litre (2 pints) vegetable or chicken stock
¾ tsp white pepper
100ml (3½fl oz) single cream
2 tbsp white miso
2 tbsp pul biber (Turkish chilli)
Sea salt

For the breadsticks:
500g (1lb 2oz) strong white bread flour, plus extra for dusting
10g (¼oz) sea salt
1 heaped tsp dried yeast
2 tbsp olive oil
350ml (12fl oz) lukewarm water
20g (¾oz) unsalted butter
1 large onion, finely sliced
150g (5½oz) potato, grated

First, make the dough. Put the flour in the bowl of a stand mixer, then add the salt to one side and yeast to the other. Add the olive oil, then gradually add the water while mixing at a slow speed. Mix for 5 minutes until smooth. Cover the bowl and leave to prove for about 1 hour, or until just doubled in size.

Meanwhile, melt the butter in a frying pan and cook the onion with a pinch of salt over a very low heat for about 40 minutes, stirring frequently, until golden and soft. Set aside to cool.

Cook the grated potato in boiling salted water for 5 minutes. Drain and cool.

Preheat the oven to 220°C/425°F/gas mark 7.

On a lightly floured surface, stretch the dough out into a rough rectangle, then scatter over the cooled onion and potato. Fold over a couple of times, then very briefly knead to work the onion and potato through the dough; it will be very sticky.

Shape into a rough sausage shape, and cut into 10 slices. Stretch each into a sausage, about 20cm (8in) in length. Don't worry too much about the shaping. Place on two greased baking trays, allowing space between, cover with a cloth and leave for 15 minutes. Bake the breadsticks for 15–20 minutes, or until golden.

To make the soup, melt 20g (¾oz) of the butter in a large saucepan over a medium heat. Add the onion and celery and cook for about 10 minutes until softened. Pour in the wine and let it bubble down until it has almost disappeared. Add the celeriac, bay leaves, stock and white pepper. Cook for 10–15 minutes, or until just tender.

Remove the bay leaves, then blend using a stick blender (or a liquidiser, but be careful only to half-fill the jug if the soup is still hot). Add the cream and blend again. Check the seasoning and add more salt and white pepper if necessary.

To serve, melt the remaining butter in a saucepan and whisk in the miso and pul biber. Swirl a spoonful on top of each mug of soup before serving with the breadsticks. Eat immediately.

BBQ ONGLET TACOS WITH PUMPKIN AND SCOTCH BONNET SALSA

Onglet is the queen of steaks, in my opinion; it should be cooked quickly, rested well and sliced very thinly. The reward is soft, rare meat with a richness and depth that's reminiscent of offal. If you're outside for Bonfire Night, the tacos can be self-assembled and are easy to eat standing up, and the steak can be cooked on a barbecue.

```
Serves 10

1.5kg (3lb 5oz) onglet
Sea salt

For the tortillas:
500g (1lb 2oz) masa harina
2 large pinches of salt
About 600ml (20fl oz) warm water

For the salsa:
1 scotch bonnet chilli, deseeded (if you like) and very finely
chopped
3-4 tbsp lime juice
1 butternut squash or Delica pumpkin (1.2kg/2lb 10oz), peeled and
cut into roughly 1cm (¾in) dice
1 small onion, very finely chopped
1 large bunch (about 100g/3½oz) coriander, finely chopped

To serve:
100g (3½oz) pumpkin seeds, toasted
Soured cream
```

First make the tortilla dough. Combine the masa and salt in a bowl and slowly add the warm water. Use your hands to bring it together into a smooth, soft dough without any lumps. Let this sit, covered or wrapped, for 30 minutes while you make the salsa.

Combine the scotch bonnet with 3 tablespoons of the lime juice in a small bowl and set aside. Cook the squash in boiling salted water for a few minutes, or until just tender. Drain and combine with the onion, coriander, chilli and lime juice, and some salt. Allow to sit for 15 minutes before tasting – add more lime juice and salt if necessary. The salsa should be zingy, and the chilli heat will mellow over time.

To make the tortillas, place a cast-iron pan or heavy-based non-stick frying pan over a high heat. Roll pieces of the dough into balls roughly the size of a golf ball. Place a square of baking paper into a taco press and put the ball on top.

Top with another sheet of baking paper and press down firmly but gently. Alternatively, you can use a rolling pin (or the palm of your hand) to shape the dough balls into rounds.

Once the pan is hot, cook the tortillas, a few at a time, for a minute or so on each side, until the edges start to look dry, then flip. They will have a speckled appearance when ready and may puff up a little when pressed. Put the cooked tortillas into a folded, clean tea towel and repeat with the remaining dough. The tortillas can sit in the tea towel, where they will stay soft and warm.

If cooking the steak on a barbecue, prepare it for direct cooking over high heat. If cooking indoors, heat a griddle pan or heavy frying pan over a high heat.

Season the steak heavily with sea salt on both sides, then cook for a few minutes on each side. Rest for 10 minutes. Slice very thinly and sprinkle with a little more salt. Serve with the tortillas, salsa, pumpkin seeds and soured cream.

WHISKY CARAMEL MILLIONAIRE'S SHORTBREAD

This is a moodier, boozier iteration of a classic, with a smoky whisky caramel and dark chocolate topping that feels appropriate for a crisp, cold evening watching fireworks (or with a cup of tea the next day). The sprinkle of salt on top is optional but good – you can also add a pinch to the caramel.

Serves 16

For the shortbread:
175g (6oz) unsalted butter, cubed
250g (9oz) plain flour
80g (2¾oz) caster sugar

For the whisky caramel:
150g (5½oz) unsalted butter
300g (10½oz) condensed milk
70g (2½oz) light brown sugar
3 tbsp golden syrup
50ml (2fl oz) whisky

For the chocolate topping:
350g (12oz) dark chocolate, broken into pieces
Flaky sea salt (optional)

Preheat the oven to 170°C/340°F/gas mark 3½. Grease and line a 23cm (9in) cake tin.

First, make the shortbread by pulsing the flour and butter in a food processor until the mixture resembles fine breadcrumbs. Add the sugar and pulse again to combine.

Tip the crumbs into the lined cake tin and spread out evenly. Press down firmly with your knuckles, until it is tightly packed and level. Bake for 30 minutes or until lightly golden. Set aside while you make the caramel.

Heat the butter, condensed milk, sugar and golden syrup in a saucepan, stirring until smooth. Bring to the boil and heat for about 5 minutes until thickened and golden brown, whisking regularly to prevent the bottom from burning. Remove from the heat and carefully whisk in the whisky. Pour the caramel over the shortbread and allow to cool completely.

To make the topping, melt the chocolate in a bowl set over a saucepan of barely simmering water (ensure the base of the bowl doesn't touch the water). Allow the melted chocolate to cool for a few minutes, then pour it over the set caramel. Sprinkle with flaky sea salt, if you like. Leave to set, then turn out of the tin and cut into portions.

Reading List

Rob Howell,
Root
Cooking through the seasons with a focus on sustainability. The spicy buttermilk-fried celeriac is a must, followed by sweet carrot jam doughnuts.

Yemisi Aribisala,
Longthroat Memoirs
Essays examining the complexities, peculiarities, meticulousness and tactility of Nigerian food.

Lope Ariyo,
Hibiscus
Bold and energetic recipes that capture the diversity of Nigerian cuisine yet experiment with flavours and ingredients from around the world.

Mallika Basu,
Masala
A fun and inventive cookbook that both dispels curry myths and offers helpful tips and easy cheats to create a true taste of India in a modern kitchen.

Asma Khan,
Asma's Indian Kitchen
A celebration of heritage, culture and community, with recipes that follow the route of the Darjeeling Express train from the busy streets of Bengal, through Calcutta and along the foothills of the Himalayas to Hyderabad.

Nina Mingya Powles,
Tiny Moons
Meditative reflections on family, solitude and belonging, intertwined with mouthwatering descriptions of noodles, dumplings and sesame pancakes.

Helen Graves,
Live Fire
Seasonal barbecue recipes celebrating live fire cooking around the world. Interviews with chefs and home cooks from the multiple diaspora communities in the UK explore the ideas and techniques that define and unite the way we grill.

December

There's a fizz of anticipation in the air as Christmas approaches. Plan parties and festive gatherings to keep out the damp and drizzle, stock the larder full of warming spices, nuts and dried fruit, and return to the rituals that bring comfort and joy. Sweeten each day with mince pies, spiced biscuits and gingerbread – now isn't the time for restraint. And whatever you serve on Christmas Day, cook with exuberance and always make sure there are leftovers.

IN SEASON

Brussels sprouts
Celery
Clementines
Dates
Kiwi fruit
Leeks
Parsnips

Persimmons
Pomegranates
Red cabbage
Swede
Walnuts
Wild onion

Walnuts

CHRISTMAS RITUALS

'They fall when ripe, and lie, like small white bones, very bright on their broken husks.' So begins Dorothy Hartley's poetic description of walnuts in *Food in England*, alongside suggestions for pickling and making pot-pourri with the sweet-smelling leaves. Grown in Britain for centuries, walnuts were used far more frequently in the past, gathered in late autumn to make pies, puddings, sauces, cakes, soups and stuffings. The best are pale and creamy (the skin darkens as the nut ages) so seek out the new harvest if you've been deterred by dry, brittle bitterness – they will be a revelation.

Walnuts are the nuts of art and feasting, their intricate curves captured by Dutch masters alongside grapes, pomegranates and pears. They adorn our Christmas fruit bowls and cheeseboards, decorative as well as delicious. In the nineteenth century, gilded walnut shells were tied with red ribbons to the upper boughs of the Christmas tree, often concealing small trinkets for New Year's Day.

The Victorians turned nutcracking into a leisurely dinner ritual, eating walnuts with wine at the end of a meal. The slow rhythm of cracking the shells and carefully removing the rough husks feels suitably ritualistic for Christmastime, when a soldierly nutcracker is often to be found nearby. And if you happen to sit by a roaring fire, wrap a handful of whole walnuts in foil, the shells cracked but not removed, and roast them to enjoy with crisp pears and a farmhouse cheese.

WHAT TO DO WITH WALNUTS

- Pair with Parma ham and honey for the simplest of starters.
- Blitz with red peppers to make the Syrian dip *muhammara* or blend with bread and plenty of garlic for Greek *skordalia*.
- Scatter on salads, especially those with bitter leaves and piquant blue cheese.
- Drizzle the intensely nutty oil on winter greens and fruit such as persimmons, apples and figs.
- Combine with Parmesan, mascarpone and garlic for a creamy pasta sauce.
- Make a chestnut and walnut pie accompanied by Cumberland sauce, the perfect centrepiece for a vegetarian Christmas lunch.
- Grind into flour to thicken French sauces, Mexican *mole* and Iranian stews, such as *fesenjan*.
- Whip up French *aillade*, the ground walnuts replacing the egg yolks of the better-known aioli, and serve with crudités.
- Caramelise to make brittle for both sweet and savoury dishes, adding a little salt and freshly ground black pepper to lift the flavour and bring a hint of spice.
- Try Hungarian *gundel palacsinta*, thin crêpe-like pancakes filled with walnuts, raisins and rum.
- Dip in dark chocolate and eat with vanilla ice cream.

MAKE AHEAD

Candied citrus peel

Keep the peel of any unwaxed citrus – orange and lemon are classics for a reason, but try clementine, kumquat and bergamot too – or simply pare the zest for a quicker, sweeter version. Simmer in water, followed by sugar syrup, then leave to dry and toss in sugar. The candied peel will keep for months, if not years, ready to be chopped into cakes and puddings. Dipping pieces into melted dark chocolate – just half looks particularly fetching – turns this store cupboard staple into a delicious gift.

Muhammara
by Anas Atassi

Muhammara originated in the Syrian city of Aleppo and variations on it are served across much of the Middle East. My love for this spicy red pepper and walnut dip is all-encompassing. I'm especially crazy about mixing it with hummus – give it a try! The secret to a good muhammara is in the red pepper paste, made with peppers that have been slowly roasted, cooled and then dried. It's worth the effort to find this paste, but it's still delicious without it. Serve as part of a mezze with flatbread, or as a sauce for grilled meats and fish.

Serves 4

150g (5½oz) roasted red peppers from a jar
1 tsp *biber salcasi* or Turkish red pepper paste (optional)
1 red chilli
75g (2¾oz) walnuts
50g (1¾oz) breadcrumbs
2 tbsp extra virgin olive oil
1 tbsp pomegranate molasses
Juice of ½ lemon
Sea salt

To serve:
Extra virgin olive oil
Pomegranate molasses
½ handful of flat-leaf parsley, coarsely chopped
½ handful of walnuts, coarsely chopped

Either pulse all the ingredients in a food processor, for about 2 minutes, or pound together using a pestle and mortar. You want to achieve a thick mixture that keeps some texture from the walnuts. This dip will keep well refrigerated, but should be served at room temperature. To serve, drizzle with extra virgin olive oil and pomegranate molasses. Garnish with chopped parsley and walnuts.

Ginger

by Pen Vogler

Our Anglo-Saxon forebears knew and valued ginger for its health-giving properties. Spices were administered by monks for the physical and spiritual health of their communities. Ginger was part of the 'coffer of treasures' that The Venerable Bede distributed to his Benedictine brethren on his deathbed in 735, and his contemporaries recommended it as a cure for hiccups.

It's not surprising that we welcome the heat of ginger in our coldest season, nor that the more luxury-loving Anglo-Normans combined it with other imported (and therefore prestigious) spices and wines. Not all medieval recipes are worth reviving, as some of my long-suffering dinner guests will attest, but *hippocras* or *ypocras* (named after Hippocrates) is a lovely mulled wine with a gingery kick that was popular for centuries. In a recipe by John Russell, steward to the Duke of Gloucester, around 1460, he gives instructions to make sure the ginger has 'good hete' (and isn't worm-eaten) and to mix it with cinnamon, cardamom, sugar and two interesting spices no longer much used: grains of paradise and long pepper. King Henry VIII and Queen Catherine enjoyed a hippocras jelly, and I recommend taking a leaf (of gelatine) out of their book, as jellies of spiced wines make wonderful Christmassy puddings.

As Russell's recipe suggests, ginger has long had friendly relations with other spices, and found itself leading the way in the 'sweetmeats' that enabled those who could afford such imported riches to show off to their guests. One early recipe has a showstopper gingerbread, decorated with gilt and studded with cloves. Eliza Acton revived this brilliant partnership with lashings of ginger and a subtle hint of cloves in her iconic 1845 recipe for gingerbread.

On wealthy medieval and Tudor tables, ginger was used in savoury food as much as in sweet – a trick learnt from the Crusaders returning from the Holy Land (and rediscovered with each generation that encountered the excitement of Indian and other Asian cuisines). Thanks to William the Conqueror's addiction to deer-hunting, venison had the highest status of all meats in post-Norman England; it came with a Christmas pottage of breadcrumbs spiced with ginger and its associates, mace, cloves, pepper and saffron. This has been passed down to us today as bread sauce, one of the Christmas 'trimmings' more glorious than the turkey.

Few cooks put ginger in bread sauce today. From Stuart times, it started to uncouple itself from aristocratic savoury dishes. As Britain's empire expanded and aggressive colonial trading practices intensified, light, easily transported, powdered ginger became more affordable and found its way into homely baking.

Every farmhouse, village and town had its own version of gingerbread, and it is a testament to the good nature of ginger that the results are so varied. It marries particularly well with oatmeal, wheatmeal, black treacle and golden syrup to enliven cakes, sponges, breads and biscuits; hefty indulgences for people who might actually be hungry. Parkin, made with oatmeal (grown in cooler, wetter northern counties and Scotland) has become anchored to Bonfire Night; the famous Grasmere Gingerbread was originally given to children as a reward (or bribe?) for bringing rushes to church. Further south, the annual agricultural fairs gave their name to the ginger fairings, a treat for the labourers who went to find work for the year ahead.

The most famous gingerbread is the fantasy house that so beguiles the starving siblings Hansel and Gretel. When the story was published by the Brothers Grimm in the early 1800s, it inspired German bakers to make elaborate *lebkuchen* houses for Christmas; a custom eagerly adopted in Scandinavia and the US, followed by Britain. The great charm of the gingerbread house is a contrast that gets to the heart of Christmas in the northern hemisphere; the suggestion of deep midwinter cold from the icing-sugar snow and the 'good hete' of invigorating, warming ginger.

ACTON GINGERBREAD

This is a modern retelling of Eliza Acton's iconic 1845 recipe from *Modern Cookery for Private Families*. 'We retain the name given to it originally in our own circle,' she writes, with justifiable pride.

Serves 10–12

175g (6oz) unsalted butter
4 eggs
4 tbsp milk
450g (1lb) self-raising flour
1 heaped tbsp ground ginger
1 tsp ground cloves
280g (10oz) black treacle or molasses
280g (10oz) golden syrup
175g (6oz) soft brown or muscovado sugar
Zest of 2 lemons
2–3 tbsp chopped stem ginger (optional)

Preheat the oven to 170ºC/325ºF/gas mark 3. Grease and line a 23cm (9in) square cake tin.

Whisk the eggs thoroughly with the milk, until they start to froth. Sift the flour and spices into a large bowl. Measure the black treacle and golden syrup into a saucepan (this is easiest to do using a metal spoon heated in hot water). Add the sugar, butter and lemon zest. Heat very gently until the butter is just melted. Pour this into a well in the flour, beating vigorously. When it is well blended, add the egg and milk mixture and the stem ginger, if using, beating well until you see bubbles forming on the surface.

Pour into the prepared cake tin and bake for about 1½ hours until firm to the touch and a skewer inserted into the centre comes out clean.

Turn out and cool on a wire rack. Store in an airtight container or wrapped in foil for a few days before eating to let the flavours develop.

A Danish Christmas

by Trine Hahnemann

In Denmark, Christmas truly begins on the first Sunday of Advent. The streets light up as the nights get longer, ornaments shimmer and sparkle in shop windows, and the scent of spiced biscuits and *gløgg* lingers in the air wherever you go.

On Advent Sundays, we meet friends and family at home, baking *brunkager* biscuits filled with nuts, buttery vanilla wreaths of *vaniljekranse*, and spiced *pepparkakor* for the days ahead. There is plenty of *hygge* as the year is ending and we celebrate the darkest day – the year is turning and brighter days will soon return.

We celebrate Christmas a day earlier than much of the world; the whole of December leading up to the big day on the 24th. Families gather together late in the afternoon for champagne or gløgg – homemade mulled wine with raisins and almonds – and toast to a wonderful *juleaften* (Christmas Eve).

The day before, I wake up early and go down to my kitchen; the whole house is quiet. I make my morning tea, light all the candles and put on Christmas music while I plan the day's cooking ahead. I always start by boiling a large portion of *risalamande*, a rice pudding traditionally served cold with cherry sauce. I wrap the pot in newspaper and a few wool blankets and leave it to rest, ready for the festive game we will play the next day. The creamy, lush pudding is full of roughly chopped almonds, except one that is left whole. If you find the whole almond, you win a prize, but first you have to hide it for as long as possible to keep the suspense and make everybody eat far too much pudding.

The traditional Christmas dinner in Denmark is roast duck, goose or pork served with gravy, red cabbage and *brunkartofler*, small boiled potatoes caramelised in sugar. On Christmas Eve, I stuff the ducks with apples, onions, prunes and thyme ready for roasting, and thicken the cherry sauce for the risalamande. I gently fold whipped cream into the pudding and season it with sugar and vanilla, keeping it cold for later. Then I set the table and get the whole kitchen up and running – steaming, boiling, spreading out happiness.

When I'm ready, I swap my apron for a festive dress and join my family for a glass of champagne, wishing everybody a *glædelig jul*. The ritual of Christmas makes me grasp time more clearly, helps me better appreciate the now. In her spirit, my *mormor* is present – warm memories of standing in the kitchen as a little girl, hands clasped around her legs, waiting to be given the simplest of tasks. I know she thought Christmas was hard work, but as a child, I never sensed that. Cooking the Christmas dinner was a ritual of love, and that feeling has always stayed with me.

Party Food
by Milli Taylor

Entertaining doesn't need to be daunting. Keep it simple and remember that less is always more.

Let's start at the beginning (when the doorbell rings and the first guest arrives 5 minutes early) and let's start small. You can't be busting out the canapés when there's only a handful of guests, or there'll be none left. Everyone loves crisps. Olive oil crisps and homemade taramasalata? Perfect. Mix things up with plantain crisps, roasted peanuts with crispy aromatic curry leaves or a bowl of *chicharrones*. Really, what I'm saying is that everyone likes salty, crunchy things and this buys you some time.

For laid-back party hosting, take a tip from the nation that does the best small eats. Spanish tapas may be simple, but if you buy the best ingredients, you have heaven on a plate. What do you eat when standing at a busy bar that needs no cooking whatsoever? A plate of glossy, green, salty, spicy *gilda*. Pick up good anchovies, pitted green olives and pickled guindilla peppers and skewer them on cocktail sticks. Leave off the anchovies for your veggie or vegan friends.

Try to pick a mix of hot and cold food. Balance the menu in terms of fresh/fried, light/filling, and contrasting flavours. This is where you can have fun and mix up cuisines. Be generous: you may not think of cooking your guests a fillet steak at a dinner party, but one steak at a canapé party will feed twenty, sliced thinly and draped over a crostini with a little mascarpone mixed with truffle porcini paste, a shaving of Parmesan and some rocket.

If you're a keen cook and fancy trying a few new canapés at Christmas, these are my all-time favourites: leek and Parmesan filo tartlets; buttery Cheddar and cayenne biscuits; lentil fritters with tamarind and pepper chutney; gougères; Stilton and pear butter toasts; aubergine curry on mini poppadoms; saltfish fritters; salmon and crème fraîche buckwheat blinis; spiced Persian sausage rolls with barberries; dates stuffed with soft goat's cheese and topped with pistachios, orange zest and pomegranate seeds.

If in doubt, pop some cheese on cocktail sticks and wrap delicious things in bacon – prunes, oysters, mini sausages, chestnuts – anything 'on horseback'. As long as your guests have a free hand to hold their festive fizz, anything goes.

A Menu for December
by Milli Taylor

DEEP-FRIED SPROUT TONNATO WITH CRISPY CAPERS

I've won over sprout sceptics with this recipe. The Brussels are a treat on their own, but it's worth going the extra mile and putting the whole dish together, especially when each component can be prepared well before serving.

Serves 4

For the pickled shallots:
1 large banana shallot
120ml (4fl oz) red wine vinegar
30g (1oz) caster sugar
Fine sea salt

For the tonnato:
1 can of tuna, 110g (4oz) drained weight
6 anchovy fillets
2 tbsp red wine vinegar
1 whole egg and 1 egg yolk
1 garlic clove
120ml (4fl oz) mild olive oil

For the sprouts:
Vegetable oil, for frying
2 shallots, sliced into thin rings
600g (1lb 5oz) Brussels sprouts, trimmed and halved
3 tbsp capers, drained

For the pickled shallots, slice off the top and bottom of the shallot and peel off the skin and the first layer, then slice into thin rounds and put in a bowl. Gently separate the layers into rings and sprinkle with a teaspoon of fine sea salt. Set aside for 5 minutes.

Meanwhile, put the vinegar and sugar in your smallest saucepan over a medium heat and bring to a simmer. Swirl the pan around for a minute or two until all the sugar is dissolved and then turn off the heat.

Cover the shallot slices with boiling water and drain. Add the shallots to the vinegar and leave to cool. Once cooled, pour into a jar and refrigerate.

For the tonnato, put all the ingredients except the olive oil in a food processor and give them a good whizz. Scrape down the sides and blend again. Leaving the motor running, slowly add the oil and blend for a couple of minutes until well emulsified. Cover and chill.

To cook the sprouts, add enough oil to a large, heavy-based saucepan to fill it to 10cm (4in) deep. Heat the oil to 175°C (345°F) and drop in the shallots. Move them around the oil with a slotted spoon and cook until golden brown. Remove with a slotted spoon and drain on kitchen paper, then set aside on a plate.

Carefully add the sprouts to the pan, working in batches (the oil might spit a bit to begin with). Cook for a few minutes, or until the outer leaves turn dark brown; they may look overcooked, but that's where the flavour is. Drain on kitchen paper, then place on a wire rack so they don't go soggy. (If you need to crisp them up before serving, you can do so in a hot oven for 5 minutes.)

Press the capers between sheets of kitchen paper and then fry until they bloom and become crisp. Drain on kitchen paper and set aside.

To serve, spoon a few tablespoons of tonnato sauce onto each plate, then scatter over the sprouts and sprinkle with a touch of salt. Drape over the pickled shallots, and then top with the fried shallots and capers.

PORK COLLAR STEAKS WITH PEAR BUTTER AND BRAISED CHICORY

Pork and apple may be the classic duo, but the sweet pear in this dish contrasts beautifully with the bitter chicory. I usually make a double batch of the pear butter and keep the leftovers for serving with a cheeseboard. Remember to marinate the steaks overnight, or for at least a few hours. You can make the beans well in advance and warm through just before serving.

Serves 4

2 thick-cut pork neck steaks
3 heads of red chicory or radicchio
15g (½oz) unsalted butter
1 tsp caster sugar
Sea salt and freshly ground black pepper

For the marinade:
3 garlic cloves, thinly sliced
2 red chillies, thinly sliced
Zest and juice of 1 large lemon
100ml (3½fl oz) extra virgin olive oil
A few thyme sprigs, leaves picked

For the pear butter:
6 large ripe Williams or Comice pears, peeled and cored
Juice of 1 lemon
½ tsp vanilla paste

For the beans:
100g (3½oz) cavolo nero, stalks removed
2 tbsp olive oil, plus extra for frying
600g (1lb 5oz) jar cooked haricot beans

4 slices of rustic bread, to serve

First make the marinade. Mix together all the ingredients, holding back a pinch of the thyme leaves. Reserve 1 tablespoon of marinade for the beans, then put the rest in a shallow dish with the steaks and marinate overnight or for at least 4 hours.

Put the pears in a food processor with the lemon juice, a splash of water and the vanilla. Blitz to combine, then transfer the mixture to a non-stick frying pan over a medium heat and stir with a spatula now and again until it reduces to a jammy paste. This will take 15–20 minutes. Keep an eye on it and add a splash of water along the way, if needed.

Meanwhile, make the beans. Put the cavolo nero in a large frying pan over a medium heat and cook for a couple of minutes with a splash of water. Add the olive oil and the reserved tablespoon of marinade and cook for another minute before adding the beans and the stock from the jar. Add another splash of water and some black pepper and cook for 5 minutes or until the beans soften. Set aside, ready to warm through later.

Heat a heavy-based frying pan over a high heat. Remove the steaks from the marinade and pat dry. Rub in a little olive oil and flaky salt and sear on both sides. You can move the steaks around and seal the sides too: they will take a good 7–8 minutes to cook overall and it's important to let the meat rest for a further 8 minutes.

Break the leaves off the chicory and fry in a hot pan in a splash of oil, then add the butter, sugar, and a pinch of the reserved thyme leaves and cook for a minute until caramelised.

Toast the bread, reheat the beans and slice the pork steaks. Pile the beans onto a big platter, then top with the chicory, pork and its resting juices Serve with the toasted bread and pear butter on the side.

DARK RUM AND PRUNE CLAFOUTIS

The addition of crème fraîche and ground almonds creates a lighter bake than a classic clafoutis. The edges fluff up like bread pudding and the custard in the middle is softly set with a gentle wibble. Leave the prunes to soak overnight so they're plump and juicy.

```
200g (7oz) Agen prunes, stoned
5 tbsp dark rum
30g (1oz) unsalted butter, plus extra for greasing
85g (3oz) caster sugar, plus 2 heaped tsp
3 medium eggs
Zest of ½ orange
30g (1oz) plain flour
40g (1¼oz) ground almonds
Pinch of salt
130ml (4½fl oz) milk
100g (3½oz) crème fraîche
15g (½oz) toasted flaked almonds (optional)
1 tsp icing sugar, for dusting
Crème fraîche or double cream, to serve
```

Place the prunes in a small bowl. Heat the rum in a small saucepan until simmering point, then pour over the prunes. Place a saucer on top and leave overnight or for at least 4 hours.

Preheat the oven to 190°C/375°F/gas mark 5. Generously grease a 20-cm (8-in) ovenproof dish with butter, then swirl 1 teaspoon of sugar around the dish.

In a large bowl, whisk together the eggs, the 85g (3oz) sugar and the orange zest until light and fluffy. Whisk in the flour, ground almonds and salt.

Melt the butter and whisk it into the batter, along with the milk and crème fraîche.

Lift the prunes out of the rum and place in the bottom of the prepared dish, then pour over the batter. I like to sprinkle the top with some toasted flaked almonds and a teaspoon of caster sugar.

Bake in the middle of the oven for 30 minutes without opening the door. After 30–35 minutes, take out the clafoutis and check that the custard is just set in the middle. The surface will deflate a little, but it's important to let the custard rest for at least 5 minutes before dusting with icing sugar and serving up with a dollop of crème fraîche or cream.

Reading List

Anas Atassi,
Sumac
A tribute to the author's homeland of Syria, told through recipes passed down the generations. As well as the *muhammara*, try the *qatayef* – mini pancakes with a sweet walnut filling.

Pen Vogler,
Scoff
A history of food and class in Britain, exploring how social status has determined what we eat today. Flick to the chapter on gingerbread.

Eliza Acton,
Modern Cookery for Private Families
First published in 1845, this bestselling masterpiece was one of the first cookery books to provide lists of ingredients, exact quantities and cooking times, establishing the format for modern cookbook writing.

Sam Bilton,
First Catch Your Gingerbread
A joyous and deeply researched collection of gingerbread recipes throughout history.

Trine Hahnemann,
Scandinavian Christmas
Spiced biscuits, *gløgg*, roast duck and *brunkartofler* – everything you need to have a *glædelig jul*.

Milli Taylor,
Party-Perfect Bites
Party snacks for every season, with fabulous ideas for festive gatherings, such as Stilton with red-wine poached pears on walnut toast, chestnuts wrapped in bacon, and rose and raspberry profiteroles.

Mollie Stanley-Wrench,
Cocktail Snacks and Canapés
A fifties classic for fans of stuff on sticks. Just avoid the sardine eclairs.

Elizabeth Price,
Hors d'Oeuvres and Appetisers
A 1977 masterwork that deserves a reprint as much for the garish photography as for the daring recipes – banana and olive skewers, neon crème de menthe jellies, or apricots stuffed with pink anchovy-flavoured cheese.

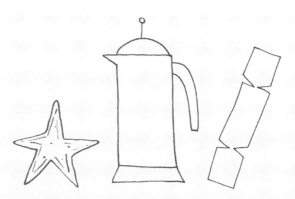

Index

Author Index

Acknowledgements

Pavilion
An imprint of
HarperCollins*Publishers* Ltd
1 London Bridge Street
London SE1 9GF

www.harpercollins.co.uk

HarperCollins*Publishers*
1st Floor, Watermarque Building
Ringsend Road Dublin 4
Ireland

10 9 8 7 6 5 4 3 2 1

First published in Great Britain by
Pavilion, an imprint of
HarperCollins*Publishers* Ltd 2022

Copyright © Miranda York 2022*

*except for all text acknowledged on
page 206

A catalogue record for this book is
available from the British Library.

ISBN 978-1-911682-24-0

MIX
Paper from
responsible sources
FSC
www.fsc.org   FSC™ C007454

This book is produced from
independently certified FSC™ paper to
ensure responsible forest management.

For more information visit:
www.harpercollins.co.uk/green

Reproduction by Rival Colour Ltd, UK
Printed and bound in China by RRD

Commissioning Editor: Sophie Allen
Project Editor: Miranda York
Designer: Will Perrens at Atwork
Illustrator: Jordan Amy Lee
Copy Editor: Stephanie Evans
Proofreader: Tara O'Sullivan
Indexer: Isobel McLean

*When using kitchen appliances please always
follow the manufacturer's instructions.*

UK/US GLOSSARY

Ingredients

aubergine – eggplant
beef fillet – beef tenderloin
beetroot – beets
biscuits – cookies
borlotti beans – cranberry beans
broad beans – fava beans
butter beans – lima beans
caster sugar – superfine sugar
celeriac – celery root
cider – hard cider
coriander (fresh) – cilantro
cornflour – cornstarch
courgettes – zucchini
double cream – heavy cream
french beans – string beans/green beans
golden syrup – *can substitute corn syrup*
icing sugar – confectioners' sugar/
powdered sugar
kitchen paper – paper towels
natural yogurt – plain yogurt
pak choi – bok choy
peppers (red/green/yellow) – bell
peppers
plain flour – all-purpose flour
porridge oats – rolled oats/oatmeal
samphire – sea beans
self-raising flour – self-rising flour
soured cream – sour cream
spring onions – scallions
stock – broth
sultanas – golden raisins
swede – rutabaga
tomato purée – tomato paste

Equipment

baking paper – parchment paper
baking tin – baking pan
cake tin – cake pan
griddle pan – grill pan
grill – broiler
kitchen paper – paper towels
muslin cloth – cheesecloth
roasting tray – roasting pan
sieve – fine mesh strainer
work surface – countertop

ABOUT THE AUTHOR

Miranda York began her career as a food, travel and culture journalist, writing for publications such as the *Financial Times, Vogue, Mr Porter* and *Harper's Bazaar* before founding At The Table, a creative platform that explores and celebrates food culture.

She has since curated over 100 events, published an independent food magazine, recorded a podcast series, produced short films and launched an artisan food market in London. In 2020, she co-founded Twelve Noon, a creative studio with an appetite for spirited stories.

Miranda was named one of Code's 100 Most Influential Women in Food and has been shortlisted for both the Jane Grigson Trust Award and the Fortnum & Mason Food & Drink Awards. The *Food Almanac: Volume II* is her second book.